NO TURNING BACK, REGARDLESS

NO TURNING BACK,

Regardless

How God Rescued Me,
Redeemed Me, and
Restored My Heart
with a Song

LISA DAGGS

with MARGOT STARBUCK

SALEM
BOOKS
an imprint of Regnery Publishing

"Sharing the stage with Lisa Daggs is always a soulful celebration! I respect and appreciate her dedication to sobriety, and her new book tells the sometimes painfully honest story of rebellion, recovery and finally, restoration. Lisa's heart for ministry is apparent on every page."

Russ Taff,
Gospel Music Hall of Famer,
winner of six Grammy Awards and fifteen GMA Dove Awards

"In *No Turning Back, Regardless,* Lisa shares the intimate details of her personal recovery story. Anyone who has been hurt in a relationship or has struggled with an addiction could relate to the deep insights revealed in this memoir. Although life takes unwanted twists and turns, Lisa's story of redemption and victory reminds us that there's always hope. Lisa's deep faith in Jesus provided the ability to persevere, the inspiration for her music, and the strength to rise above difficult circumstances. Having walked with Lisa through a good part of this story, I'm happy that she has shared it so openly and elegantly, and believe it will be an inspiration to all who read it."

Anthony Albanese MD,
president, California Society of Addiction Medicine

"Behind every star there is a story, but not one like Lisa Daggs's. From almost total self-destruction to a life of meaning, purpose and transformational love, her thirty-year journey is the path you have probably been looking for if you need some hope, help, or encouragement. If you don't think you need it, I know you know someone who does. *Regardless* provides the way for anyone to move out of the shadows of life and into the spotlight of God's love and authentic relationships. Read it and be amazed at how bad it can get, and how amazing life becomes when the steps of restoration and recovery are full of God's grace and love, regardless of what you have done."

Stephen Arterburn,
Founder of New Life Ministries and Women of Faith,
bestselling author with more than thirteen million books in print

"Lisa Daggs's powerfully honest story of traps along the journey and most importantly the hope in the way out is riveting! What a story! What a testimony! I could not stop reading!"

Devon O'Day,
Host of WSM Radio's *Nashville Today,* author and hit songwriter

ISBN: 978-1-62157-972-4

Ebook ISBN: 978-1-62157-979-3

Published in the United States by
Salem Books, an imprint of Regnery Publishing
A Division of Salem Communications
300 New Jersey Ave NW
Washington, DC 20001
www.salembooks.com

Manufactured in the United States of America

2019 Printing

Books are available in quantity for promotional or premium use. For information on discounts
and terms, please visit our website: www.regnery.com.

THIS BOOK IS DEDICATED TO:
MY FAITHFUL PRAYER WARRIOR,
MY SWEET MAMA.
APRIL 26, 1926 - JUNE 6, 2019
I WILL ALWAYS LOVE YOU.

Contents

Acknowledgements

First and foremost, my life and gratitude are due to my loving God, Who sent His Son for even me. He was patient in my running and fiercely committed to woo me back to my full God-given purpose. What gracious love is this? Thank you, Lord, for always keeping Your protective hand on me, even when I failed You so many times, and now for such a time as this—fulfilling my dreams, allowing me to reach out to the wounded, and carrying me through every step of the way. I've been in Your ministry for nearly thirty years via music and testimony. You have given me back this book endeavor; ten years after I started it and believed my life was over, You showed up again with an even better finish to the story.

Queen Ilene: Mama, Ilene Verle, Grammy, spiritual giant, and precious personal prayer warrior. You have shown by example what it is to be like Jesus, to everyone in your family and everyone you came into contact with. Through the pain of your own rejection and disappointments in life, you trusted the Lover of your soul and were guided and directed by His word. YOU prayed me back. You prayed hundreds back. You prayed this ministry into existence. Thank you for being patient, yet speaking the truth to me in strong, direct love. I could never pay you back for what you've given me. I can only try to honor you by picking up where you left off and seeing how many I can lead out of addiction and sin and into the Father's hands. It was my honor to take care of you in your last days, however excruciatingly painful to watch—the longest goodbye but a sacred time for us.

I celebrate your life! What a legacy you have left, Mama! Your crown must be somethin'. You always did like bling!

Faith Ilene: My beautiful only child and daughter. You are my heart. How I longed for a girl each time I was pregnant, through the miscarriages—and then God answered my prayers in blessing me with you. My wildly talented, soft-hearted, unique gift with a strong will. And yes, you tested that will at every turn, and I did my best to lead you through to safety. Thank you for sharing me with younger people who needed extra help. I am eternally grateful for your plea for me NOT to go to Nashville that day. I canceled immediately and we spent the last four days with Grammy and her failing health together. Singing, praying, reading, loving to the end. When I fell apart you held me up; when the waves of sorrow started to encompass you, I held you in safety. You were and are my treasure, my priority in life and in ministry. I'm looking forward to being there for you in whatever God directs you to. I couldn't love you more.

My incredible Ronnie: Thank you, dear one, for showing me what a man of God looks like. A few decoys crossed my path but the day you opened your mouth to sing, you had my attention. I'd heard the song a million times before, but not like that. I couldn't deny the anointing of God that morning. Months later as we became friends, we grew to know each other and build trust in a godly way. You were always on time—I mean, early. (Because you said, "If you're early you're on time, if you're on time your late, and if you're late . . . well . . . You're fired!" LOL)

I'm so glad I said, "Yes!" I'm excited about what God has for us in this new venture. Thank you for loving God and me a very close second. I love you, Ronnie. I'm finally home.

And then there's you: Family, friends, friends closer than family, some favorite pastors, church family, ministry partners, producers, songwriters, musicians, those that cheered me on, and who brought me into your churches to minister. Lowell and Connie Lundstrom, who took their chance on me in my very early sobriety with just a recommendation from sweet MaryAnn Cole; Bill and Gloria Gaither, who took me out on the road with them for many years. Even though I colored a little outside the lines, they loved and accepted me. They *saw* me. They *knew me and my heart*. I'm forever grateful for all the support that has come my way. For those sweet souls who showed up to help me with Mama when she stroked out on my kitchen floor in 2008 and then have circled back through to help in this long journey.

I never could have done this alone—without Jesus and His saints, without you. I pray you enjoy reading my story and somehow find yourself in between the pages. I pray you find the strength to make a change if you feel the longing to do so. It's a "We Program," this thing called life. Reach out. Be brave.

I, indeed, am a life that's been changed because of His great love . . . regardless.

Eternally Grateful,
Lisa Ilene Daggs

Foreword

Everyone is a story—a living, walking, morphing story. DNA, environments, relationships, accidents, and choices: all these combine to make us the persons we are. We can't choose the combination of chromosomes we inherit. We have little to say about the circumstances of our conceptions, the place and surroundings of our birth, or our early childhoods. Some relationships are a given; some are chosen. Accidents of physical, psychological, emotional, or spiritual happenings, it seems, either play us for the victim or become true blessings that come unearned and undeserved.

The amazing thing is that somehow, at the point of our surrender to the God Who made us and has been there all along, this Creator takes all we bring—good and bad—and makes "something beautiful of our lives." He never has a Plan B. When we turn over to Him our willful control of the things we never controlled in the first place, He transforms these frazzled strands, incredibly weaving them into Plan A, a work of grace so beautiful it takes our own breath away sometimes when we look into the mirror of His love.

Lisa Daggs is a story. She is quite a miraculous story, too, given the fact that some of her choices along the way could have—maybe should have—killed her. Sometimes it takes a lot to get our full attention. But for all of us, what in looking back seems like a random, tangled mess, God is working "for our good" into something unique in all the world. Lisa is a beautiful child with a new heart. She is still in progress, like the rest of us, and there are some areas that are still tender to the touch—but the scars are fading and strong, new tissue is forming where the gashes used to be. What is emerging is a new song that is sweeter, more melodious, and more captivating than ever.

No matter what our personal histories have been, Lisa's story is an invitation to become a fellow pilgrim, journeying alongside her in this adventure to who we are intended to be. There is joy in this journey because we watch, literally with bated breath, the alchemy of this Savior as He takes the stack of straw we have to offer and turns it into the gold of grace—both received and in turn offered to someone else who may just be hanging on for dear life.

Gloria Gaither
Lyricist and fellow pilgrim

Chapter 1

NASHVILLE, ON MY TERMS

From my first breath, all I've ever wanted to do was sing. At the center of my plan stood pure determination: I *would* be a big success. I *would* be the next big something.

If your dream is to be a movie star, you move to Hollywood. If you're a singer, you move to Nashville. It's the city of unlimited optimism. Everyone wants to make it big in Music City, USA. The bus station is packed with girls in cowboy hats, sheet music and lipstick tucked into purses and duffle bags. Half the people in the airport are dressed in black, carrying a guitar. It seems like every dishwasher, store clerk, taxi driver, and bellman is working on a demo, singing in clubs, or moonlighting in a band. The line of hopefulness forms in Nashville. It stretches around the block and extends halfway to Mississippi. But I was determined to emerge from the pack and make it big.

To pay the bills I worked as a waitress. I worked at a TGI Friday's in Sacramento, where I grew up, and the job transferred straight across when I moved to Nashville shortly out of high school. One night after my shift ended, a bartender named Buddy, the head kitchen manager, Ambry, and my friend, Belinda, went with me out back of the restaurant to shoot the bull and unwind. It was close

1

to 1 a.m., summertime, and we sweltered in Nashville's humid night air. We sat on a brick planter near a side street. The area was flanked by office buildings, another restaurant, and a funeral home. It felt pretty safe.

Out from the shadows stepped two men. They strolled up to us, hands in pockets. One was tall, about six feet, the other a little shorter. They just looked like average guys.

"You know anybody who's still serving food around here?" one of them asked.

"Try Tony Roma's across the street," I said. "If you hurry you can still make it."

Suddenly two nickel-plated guns flashed in our faces. The first man grabbed my arm and jammed his pistol in my ribs. The other man wedged his under Belinda's jaw. "We don't want anything to eat," the first man said, "but you're all going to take a walk with us." They started pushing us down the street.

The men began their inventory, still on the move. "Give us your jewelry," said the first, his hand like a vice on my arm.

We started taking off whatever we had. They rummaged through my purse and yanked out my tips from the night, about $150 cash. Everyone else handed over money, watches, and jewelry. Belinda worked for Kay Jewelers. She took off an expensive necklace and gave it to the men. I wasn't going down as easily. I had just bought a Toyota Celica off the showroom floor and clutched the keys tightly in my hand, hoping they wouldn't notice. This was our hard-earned stuff they were taking.

"Look—why don't you just get a job?!" I said.

"We do have jobs," said the man gripping me. "We're your local robbers."

I know now it was foolish not to keep my mouth shut. After about twenty yards they herded us off the main street and down an alley. The anger I felt instantly morphed into fear. Out in the open, I doubted if they actually would have pulled the trigger. It was a robbery, yes, but at worst it meant a lost car. Back in the alley, all was dark. Horrible thoughts raced through my mind. We were going to be raped. Maybe shot. Probably both.

Abruptly, we heard a screech and a crash. It's hard to fully explain the randomness of the moment. Apparently a car, seemingly by chance, had careened out of the Tony Roma's parking lot and collided with a parked car. The noise made our heads jerk around. From the alley, we could see steam rising from the first car's crumpled grill. It was all the jolt we needed.

The men with guns were gone in an instant, fleeing what was bound to become a scene. The crashed car squealed its tires, trying to back up and free itself from the parked one. Our robbers sprinted to the end of the alley and leaped over a fence.

I started chasing down the alley after them, screaming, "Hey! Give us our stuff back!"

I have no idea what I would have done if I caught them. Suddenly realizing how recklessly I was behaving, I darted behind a tree, peeking out to glimpse their car as they were taking off. It was a station wagon. A green Dodge Monaco with a discolored passenger-side door. I recognized it from the shape of its trunk.

We filed a report that night. The police asked us to return the next morning and leaf through mug shots.

At first light I phoned my mother. "You'll never believe what happened," I said.

"Tell me," she said. Her voice quavered.

I told her.

"Lisa—what time did the car accident take place?" she asked. "The one that prompted the men to run away?"

"It was about 1:20," I said.

"Lisa," my mother said. "Last night I was completely fast asleep, and the Lord woke me up with a start. You were heavy on my heart— far more strongly than usual. I walked to the other bedroom, got on my knees, and began to pray for your safety. When I finished praying I looked at the clock. It was 11:20 p.m. in California—that's 1:20 a.m. your time."

Later that morning my three friends and I returned to the police station. We were separated so we couldn't influence each other and told to look through pictures. We each identified the same men. An officer gathered us back together. His face was grave as he recounted information about the men. Ten days earlier they had robbed two couples in the same location that we had been robbed, at the end of the alley. The men had shot and killed one of the husbands. Easily, it could have gone the same way with us.

Two weeks later I was heading for a club, still fresh from the whole robbery ordeal. I was just driving down the street when I spotted a green station wagon with a discolored passenger-side door. I slowed for a closer look and saw one of the men who'd robbed us. His was a face I'd recognize anywhere. It was just a glance but our eyes locked: the devil and I. Waving his hand, he motioned me over. A fear grabbed me like never before. My foot did this weird thing on the pedal, just tapping and trembling. Struggling against my own body, I finally accelerated up the street, not looking back.

Some time later, when I was sure I wasn't being followed, I stopped in at another club and phoned the police. I was afraid to leave. I kept looking over my shoulder. I don't remember how long I stayed, but it's a safe bet that I turned to alcohol, my close companion—and a lot of it that night—for self-medication.

* * *

I had accepted Christ as a young girl, but I had drifted far from the faith and security of my childhood. Deep within my soul was an ache so wrenching it threatened to tear me apart. Somehow I had convinced myself that the only time I felt good was when I was loaded.

At the Nashville Friday's I crafted a drink called the Daggwood, named by bartenders in honor of my last name, not the cartoon character. Dagwood Bumstead never would have been able to stomach such a drink. The drink was comprised of Absolute Vodka on the rocks with a splash of cranberry juice and two quartered, squeezed lemon wedges. Liquid fire—that's how a Daggwood felt going down. Normally, one shot equals one ounce. Each of my signature beverages contained the alcohol content of three drinks, and I regularly downed three to four Daggwoods in an evening—the total equivalent of twelve shots. I'd be pretty lit but I'd still carry on.

Cocaine was everybody's favorite, and it became mine too. When you've got cocaine everybody wants to be your friend, and while it's in your pocket it creates a sense of false power. A group of us would head back to my apartment, I'd locate my bag where it was hidden, chop it up on a huge mirror, and we'd all gather around. My presentations were often creative. Sometimes it was dumped out in a big X. Sometimes in huge parallel lines. A favorite was a huge inverted furrow that stretched from one corner of the mirror to the other. These were enormous amounts too, not the pencil lines you typically see on TV. For us, a yardstick-sized stretch of coke was common. We'd hand out straws to everybody and announce in giddy voices: "Okay, ready, set, go!" Everybody would race to the center, snorting it up like fleshy vacuum cleaners.

At first the coke sizzles in your nose, then it hits hard. The drug blasts inside your brain, an immediate shot of adrenaline. Instantly everything's up close. You're hyper-alert to your surroundings. You're not hungry they way you are with pot, so cocaine is always a popular drug with women trying to stay skinny. You move fast. Talk fast. You're immediately on the chase. And you can never get enough. You always want more. You want to snort the first mound, then snort another. A little line is never enough to satisfy.

Oh, it's a glamorous life, all right. Usually no one can find a straw, so someone pulls out a dollar bill and rolls that up. You don't want to ruin any more money than you have to, so everyone passes around the same bill. The bill is wadded up and dirty from being jammed in some guy's pocket, and germy from all the hundreds of unwashed hands that have touched the bill before you. After a few passes the bill grows soggy from everybody's snot. But you keep snorting.

Then the coke is gone and everyone is sad, even in the midst of the high. You can't waste one precious speck. So everyone licks their fingers and rubs them on the mirror to get up all the dust. Soon the mirror is slimy soon from everybody's saliva, but you keep sticking the same fingers in your mouth.

Then you sit there with your leg tapping, or you pace around the room, laughing hysterically, and you feel this familiar warm trickle running down the inside of your nose. It's the same bloody ooze you've tried to stop before and soon it's a gusher. Coke penetrates your membranes, eating away the lining of your nose. Your body tries to heal but you keep throwing poison in it. Blood vessels get too big and keep bursting. Several times I had to rush to the doctor to get my nose cauterized.

The redeeming moment in the midst of our highs—ironic as the surroundings were—was that time and time again, something spiritual was brought up in conversation. Someone would mention going to Sunday School when she was a kid, or how once she prayed at summer camp, or how a neighbor lady used to give her cookies and tell her Bible stories on a flannel graph. It was such a crazy scene: we'd sit in our desperation, fried as we were, and talk about God. Surely there had to be something that was behind everything—someone who dreamed it all up and started it all. Surely there was a reason for life. Surely there was some place good to go to when we died. Sometimes I was so high I didn't remember the next day who I had been talking to.

When I relive those scenes now, there's a trembling I can't cease in my body. Once, in the midst of all the drugs and booze and snot, I received a card from my mother. "Dear Lisa, God's love is always there," she wrote. "There is no place you can go to get away from Him. There's nothing you can do that makes it so you can't come back to Him. He will always extend His love to you."

It was one of those cards you want to get from your mother but you also wish you hadn't received. You know it's truth, but the truth makes you so uncomfortable you could scream.

* * *

I was convinced that Nashville was my promised land. I wasn't leaving.

Home for me became the area known as Music Row. Centered around 16th and 17th Avenues South, along with several side streets, Music Row is widely considered the heart of Nashville's entertainment industry. Walking down the street you see sign after famous sign: United Artist Towers. RCA. MCA. Capital Records. SONY. SESAC. ASCAP. BMI. You see record labels, publishing houses, licensing firms, recording studios, writer rooms, radio networks, radio stations.

I pounded the pavement, knocking on doors, pitching demos, holding listening sessions, always longing to run into somebody who knew somebody who could help me climb a notch. In the middle of Music Row, displayed as a symbol of all I hoped to achieve, sat Starstruck Studios, Reba McEntire's company, with its helicopter pad on top and cast iron horses rearing up out front. And then there was the temple of all I worshipped, the Ryman Auditorium, the mother church of country music, the original site of the Grand Ole Opry.

There were just enough glimmers of hope to keep me going. Plenty of big names stopped by at Friday's. Glen Campbell was a regular. Bryan Adams dropped in whenever he came to town. I served Huey Lewis, Lorrie Morgan, Marty Stuart, Waylon and Jessie Colter, Wynonna Judd and her mother Naomi. One day a legendary jazz and R&B artist whom I'll call John, four decades my senior, sat down in my section of the restaurant. My breath caught in my throat. I hurried over to take his drink order.

"Orange juice," he said, his voice sultry. At least, that's what I thought he said.

He smirked deeply when I returned with the beverage.

"That's not what I ordered, honey—I said I want some of *yo' juice.*" He ran his eyes down my legs. Reddening, I took the drink back.

We chit-chatted throughout the meal. I was a singer, I told him. I had some songs. John handed me his phone number when he went to pay his bill. He was staying at the Spence Manor, he said, an old hotel down on Music Row.

I'm a smart girl, I thought. *I can work this and not get into trouble.* At 1 a.m. I finished my shift, clocked out, and headed for the nearest payphone.

"Who's this?" said the voice over the phone.

"It's Lisa," I said, "Lisa Daggs. We met at the restaurant tonight. You said you might listen to some of my songs—remember?"

There was a long pause. "Nah, I'm really not feeling too well tonight. Maybe some other time—"

"Please, sir," I stammered. "Can I bring you something? Some aspirin maybe?"

Another long pause. John cleared his throat. "Well, maybe just a couple of Sprites," he said.

I bought two Sprites then headed to the Spence Manor. Lightly, I knocked on his door. No answer. I knocked again, a bit louder. Still nothing. Gingerly, I leaned the Sprites against the door and left. At least he would know I had come by. The next day I called him again. This time he was much more direct. "Yeah, why don't you swing around sometime today," he said. I gathered my briefcase, cassettes, and portfolio, and hurried over.

I was passionate about music. I wanted this icon to know this— he was a man of many connections. My specialty was country/blues with a rock edge. It's the music of life and relationships, love lost, love gained. It's feel-good, feel-bad, feel-with-me, let's-go-out-tonight music. I've been told I sound like Bonnie Raitt, Trisha Yearwood, Wynonna Judd, maybe even Barbara Mandrell. I have an alto voice— lower than most women. It's full, too. Clear and bold. I'm not quite five feet, five inches tall if I stretch, and music execs would often say things like, "Where's this big voice coming from such a little body?"

"Hey-ey-ey-ey," John said as he opened his hotel room door. He wore a baby blue silk robe. "Make yourself at home. I'm just getting ready for a meeting. Here, have a seat over on the bed."

I sat down. "Sir, uh, I was hoping you could listen to a few of my songs."

He took my cassettes, set them on the coffee table, and went into the bathroom, leaving the door open. "Yeah, sure," he said. "Tell me again what you do?" He squeezed toothpaste on his toothbrush and ran water into the sink. I blabbed away. I watched him brush his hair, lather his face, shave, then pat his face with a towel. Still blabbing, I must have been glancing to my right—around the room, the open suitcases, the hotel lamp, the TV in the corner—because when I looked back at him, all I saw was the baby blue silk robe. This time the robe was open and he was standing in front of me. He nodded.

There's such power when you're singing on stage. Everybody's watching you. You're the center of attention. You think you must be special because they're all standing there, clapping, whistling, cheering. You feel so important. That's certainly not how I felt in front of this renowned performer. I felt scared, small, foolish. *As if he really wanted to hear my music.*

I tried to sound nonchalant, like this sort of thing happened every day. "Uh, I just remembered I need to phone a girlfriend," I said. "You mind if I use your phone?" I pretended to call someone then made an excuse to leave. I struck the elevator button repeatedly, just wanting to put it all behind me. The next day I related the story to a few girlfriends at Friday's. "Why didn't you go for it?" one said. "That was your big chance. If you'd had his kid, you would have had it made."

I didn't want to make it in the business like that. I had made a lot of compromises in my young life already, but I would never lie down for a contract. At least I had promised myself *that*.

Nashville is a city of huge hopes. Nashville can also become a city of huge disappointments. After a few years there, I classified myself as a working musician, although I still kept my day job—I was a bartender now, not a waitress anymore. Regularly I sang in studios for other people, mostly songwriters who wanted their music demoed for other artists. I performed at a lot of open-mic nights at clubs. Critics applauded me for my "crystalline voice and warm, natural rapport with audiences." I continued to go to different record companies and have them listen to my music. I was in a girls' four-piece vocal band called Heartland. We performed at a variety of gigs, including one big break where we sang at the Nashville Palace stage—at the time, one of the largest, coolest clubs in the city. There were some successes, but I certainly hadn't arrived at the place I wanted to be. In my honest moments I knew my life wasn't turning out the way I had dreamed it would. My strategy of pure determination was letting me down.

I couldn't shake an underlying feeling that there had to be more. Again and again in my mind, I replayed the night of the robbery and my mother's prayer. Though it would be years before I'd truly come to understand the length and depth and breadth of God's love for me, I found myself remembering that incident when I wondered if God cared for me. Even when my life was undone, God's steadfast faithfulness never let me go.

For some reason, for some greater purpose, God wanted me alive.

Chapter 2

WHEN I STARTED DANCING

So why was God was keeping me alive?

You've got to understand a bit of a person's history to know why she's the way she is today, so I want to take you back and tell you some of the stories about where I came from that mark me, for better or worse. To me, it's always been a wonder I was even born in the first place.

My parents had two children before me, Larry and Tim. Tim's birth gave my mother a lot of problems. Doctors warned my parents about trying again, but Mom really wanted a girl. One day when she was about three months pregnant with me, Mom was hanging clothes on the line and clutched her abdomen, doubling over from the pain. Dad was at work. A neighbor rushed her to the emergency room. "Early labor," a doctor said, and put her on strict bed rest from then on. More problems in the pregnancy were soon diagnosed. Doctors detected a lack of oxygen in my tissues and organs. They were sure I was going to be born a "blue baby," a condition in which not enough blood circulates through the body. The survival rate for blue babies at the time was about 50 percent. I could have gone either way. As my due date approached, medical staff prepared blood transfusions for me, expecting the worst.

I surprised them all. "Ilene, we got our girl," said the doctor to my mom when I was born. Nurses put away the blood transfusion equipment. I was completely healthy.

I was also full of determination. I'd need plenty of it later on, but as a kid it was almost more than I could handle. At eight months old I climbed out of my crib, eager to get a running start at the world. I fell on my head and blackened both eyes. The doctor instructed my mom to keep me up all night because I had a concussion. Black coffee would do the trick. Mom filled my bottle with the bitter stuff. I slurped it up. I've wondered as an adult if I have a gene that predisposes me to crave all things chemical. But even that would not have excused the things that were to come.

At age three I had loose blonde curls that fell to my shoulders. In spite of my strong streak, Mom describes me as a happy, compliant child. I gave hugs and cuddles to everyone I met. One day at the grocery store I had wandered off after a man commented to my mom about how darling I was. She frantically left her grocery cart and went on a sprint to find me. When she ran out the front door of the grocery store he was handing me to a woman in his car. Mom yelled, "What are you doing?!" His response, " I just wanted to show her to my wife!" I have often wondered where my life would be today had he succeeded.

My mom said I never met a stranger, and it is still true to this day! Every time I opened my mouth I was singing. My parents attended a small church in Madera, California, where we had moved shortly after I was born. The year I was three they held a "Daggs Day" at our church. Even though Dad wasn't there much, we were all well enough known to warrant a special Sunday named in our honor. Dad sang in a men's trio on Daggs Day. Mom sang in the choir. Larry, age twelve, read a poem. Tim, five, rang the church bell. I sang my first solo. They pulled the piano bench up to the pulpit mic and I climbed on top to reach it. I still remember all the words to the song. I perched one hand on my hip, pointed the finger of my other hand, and chirped out:

I love to go to Sunday School,
And I love to sing my song.
I have a way to bring them in,
Listen and I'll tell you how.

Tell 'em on the highways, tell them on the byways
Tell 'em that you're their friend.
Tell 'em the church is open
They're welcome to drop in.

Sing just a little bit, talk just a little bit
Throw in a smile or two,
Heavy on the howdy do,
For the Lord is a-countin' on, the Lord is a-countin' on, the
*   Lord is a-countin' on you.*

About two hundred people were in the pews that morning. They erupted in a standing ovation. I was a roaring success. At age three, I was on my way.

It wasn't all smooth sailing. A few weeks later we were all in the car on the way home from church. As we rounded an intersection in heavy traffic, I was fiddling with the door handle. The door flew open, sending me flying out into the street. I bounced and rolled, a tiny blonde ball of human road kill. Dad slammed to a stop. Everyone jumped out, sure I was a goner. My brothers yelled. Bystanders screamed. Dazed, I stood up, clutching the hem of my dress. My mom grabbed me and kept running her hands all over me, checking for bruises, cuts and broken bones, incredulous that I was still in one piece. An eyewitness told her our car's back tire had been just inches from my stomach.

A few years later it happened again. My mom and dad were both working then, and a neighbor lady watched me after school. One day as she drove me home the back door flew open as we rounded a corner—even though this time I wasn't touching the handle at all—and I bounced out of the moving car. It's almost unthinkable that I'd fly out a moving car twice as a child. This time I hit my head, scraped my back along the pavement, and ended up in the gutter. The neighbor lady screeched to a stop, scooped me up, scraped and bleeding, and raced me to my parents' house. Everyone was screaming. The woman who lived across the street tore into the lady who watched me. "What were you thinking? What were you thinking?" she kept repeating. They checked me over for broken bones and cleaned up my back. No one could believe that—again—I had walked away from the accident, virtually unharmed.

Years later I've thought it an ironic twist that I landed in the gutter. It wouldn't be the last time.

* * *

Despite my accidents, much of my childhood was filled with tenderness. I loved church and Sunday School. I loved the songs and hymns, the Bible stories, the people of all ages who crouched down to my level in the foyer to hug me or shake my hand after service was over. The cross, the grave, the resurrection—it all sounded good to me. I don't remember exactly where I was or what I prayed, but I know my decision was real. Following my mom's leading, I opened my heart to Christ and vowed to follow Him always.

I never wanted sins to collect in my life. Anytime I became aware of the slightest wrongdoing I'd pray that Christ would forgive me. I worried that if I died and I hadn't confessed all my sins up to date I wouldn't go to Heaven. I'd pray and pray, always desperate for mercy. About the time I became a Christian I joined the community swim team. Freestyle and breaststroke were my favorites. They taught us to get up on the blocks, get on our marks, grab the box, crouch and go, then extend our bodies and reach for the other side of the pool. I loved the feel of the water, the unrestricted movement in the pool. All my friends in the neighborhood joined and we raced together. I got a lot of second- and third-place ribbons, but I always wanted the blue.

For some reason all the rest of the girls on the team had better-looking swimsuits than mine. At least that's how it seemed. We all wore the same red one-piece Speedos. One day in the changing room I spied Susan Taylor's swimsuit lying on a bench. Glancing around to make sure no one was looking, I stuffed it into my swim bag. Susan's mother came to our house that night. Did I know anything about her daughter's suit? I swore I didn't. The swimsuit was mine—over and over I insisted—but Mom knew she hadn't bought that suit for me. She handed it over to Susan's mother, apologizing on my behalf. I stayed in my lie, never conceding the truth. I wasn't proud of it. Even at age seven I knew what truth was.

Trouble has a way of bursting out of you, circling your life, and coming back into it. When I was in fourth grade, we lived across the street from school, and every day I went home for lunch. Once when I came back to school after lunch was over, I spotted my best friend Tammy doing hand claps with another girl:

Miss Mary Mack, Mack, Mack,
All dressed in black, black, black
with silver buttons, buttons, buttons,
all down her back, back, back . . .

I couldn't bear the thought of Tammy having another best friend. I was her best friend. So I pushed the other girl out of the way and took her position in front of Tammy. I've always had an insecure streak. My teacher, Mrs. Slater, found out about the pushing incident and called me up in front of the class. She was very straight-faced, with short hair and a big curl up front that vibrated with every step she took. I was a "very mean girl," she announced. I was "very, very bad. Horrible. Awful. Wicked." She picked me off the ground and shoved me into the side of the classroom's piano. "How would you like it if I pushed you?" my teacher snarled. My eyes were as big as silver dollars. Tammy ran out of the class in tears, back over to my house across the street—it frightened her so much she had to hide. We found her later in our trash can, the lid clamped tightly down.

Whatever childhood troubles came my way, I always found refuge in music. It was always there, welcoming, never disappointing, always joyful. I sang all the time—in my bed at night, in front of the mirror, in a grade school operetta called *Mulligan's Magic*. I joined the school choir and band as soon as I was allowed. Mom bought me violin and viola lessons. But what I really wanted was a piano. A piano is everything to someone who loves music. With a piano, you can fly.

One day at recess I looked across the street to our house and saw a huge moving van out front. I left the game of Four Square I was playing with my friends and stuck my nose through the chain-link fence at the school's edge. The movers set down a ramp right up the front steps to our house. Out from the truck they wheeled it: a beautiful, caramel-wood, upright piano. My parents didn't see me, standing where the bikes were parked by the fence, but I knew that piano was for me.

I started lessons immediately. Plunking around was always a lot more fun than practicing a lesson, and I found I had a knack for creating the sounds I wanted to hear. Soon Mom announced that she wasn't going to remind me to practice my lessons anymore. From then on, it was mostly musical self-discovery. Mom and Dad had a huge collection of hip, bluesy, vinyl records and eight-tracks: Tony Bennett, Dusty Springfield, Burt Bacharach, Ralph Carmichael. I devoured them all. One Christmas after we had moved to Sacramento, our church hosted a huge singing Christmas tree downtown at Memorial Auditorium. In addition to the singing tree were a lot of special acts. Two friends and I sang a trio one evening, and a picture of us made the newspaper, all with our mittens and scarves on.

I loved the intensity of the night, the nerves and anticipation beforehand, then the warmth of the bright lights, the height of the performance, the affirmation once the song was all over. I loved it all.

* * *

My dad was in the audience that night. I'm sure he must have clapped for me. I'm sure he said something on the way home, but I don't remember it. With Dad, I only remember hoping.

Dad was always a mix of charm and ruse. Mom was the faithful one in the house. When we lived back in LA, Mom and Dad were involved in the church a bit, mostly because Mom did the dragging and Dad acquiesced. They let Dad collect the offering each Sunday. His gambling buddies called him Dirty Deacon Daggs. One Sunday night Mom and Dad got into a low-murmured argument in the living room. We kids never heard them fight out loud. It wasn't until years later I found out what that scrap was about. Dad was supposed to take the offering to the bank that Sunday—all $590 of it. He had gambled it instead and lost everything.

There was more to Dad's habit we didn't know much about. Mom worked as a waitress when we were little. She had saved her tips for some time and bought herself an O'Keefe & Merritt stove, something she had always dreamed of owning. One day some men in a truck came and took Mom's prize stove away. We never knew exactly why, but Dad hadn't worked in a couple of months. He had been out most nights with friends, playing some sort of card game. We suspected it had something to do with that.

I was quite willing to overlook any shortcomings Dad might have had. I worshipped him, as many little girls do with their fathers: he was my hero. When he was home I tried to hang around him as much as possible. He let me sit on his foot as he walked through the house. Constantly I sought his approval, and whenever he reprimanded me it sent me reeling. One time, when I was about three,

I leaned in to kiss him as he held me, my mouth slightly open, and he recoiled suddenly, "Never do that again," he said, jerking me as far away from me as his arms could reach. "Always keep your mouth closed. Always!" His eyebrows were lowered and tense. What had I done? I had no idea why Daddy considered that so bad. I just wanted to be his little girl. I just wanted to climb in his lap and be held close. I was only three; what did I know?

Dad ran a hamburger joint known for its delicious fries, inexpensive cheeseburgers, and ice cream sundaes. He opened another restaurant after we moved to Sacramento. Pretty soon he had a chain of six restaurants called Smorgy Boys. Money must have been coming in from somewhere because soon my mom drove a gold Lincoln Continental and dad drove a cool red T-Bird, and we still had our station wagon and gold Ford Mustang. You always assume your parents have a solid relationship, but it's funny what they can hide from you.

One day out of the blue Mom announced to us kids that we were leaving for Disneyland. It was just her and Tim and me going (being the eldest, Larry was out of the house by then)—for some reason Dad wasn't coming along. That sounded okay to my ears, but I couldn't understand why she wasn't smiling at the thought of going to Disneyland. She packed up our car with an unusual amount of clothes, bags, suitcases. We crammed ourselves in. Mom checked us into the Disneyland Hotel, which was an unexpected treat. Tim and I screamed up and down the Big Thunder Mountain Railroad, sang along at It's A Small World, and strolled down Main Street USA. Mom seemed to spend a lot of time on the phone talking to a neighbor back home. After four days we packed up and returned to Sacramento. Our house looked immaculate. Everything was dusted and vacuumed. All the dishes sparkled. Dad met us all at the door with a weak smile. "Just glad to have you back," he said to Mom—it sounded like a funny greeting to me.

Dad's life contained a lot of mysteries. On Thanksgiving Day when I was eight years old, everything was set for our feast at home.

The turkey was crackling along nicely in the oven. Mom was busy in the kitchen making pumpkin pie, and I was helping everywhere I could. Dad came into the living room where we kids were playing a game and said he felt like taking a little drive—why didn't we all come along? We kids piled in. Mom said something about being thrown off schedule, but shook her head, untied her apron, and got her coat. We just started driving. Dad wouldn't tell us where we were going. Maybe he didn't know. Two hours later we arrived in Lake Tahoe. Dad walked into a casino. Mom phoned the neighbors and asked them to turn off our oven. That night we slept in a luxurious hotel. The next day Dad took us to a ski resort and slapped down cash for new skis, boots, poles, bindings, jackets, pants, hats, gloves, lessons—everything—for all of us. We didn't know how much Dad had won the night before, but he was in a great mood. He certainly didn't announce it and Mom, with a brokenhearted smile, didn't say a word.

One day at home Mom told me she didn't want me answering the phone anymore. When I asked why, she pressed her lips together and shook her head. Funny what kids can overhear, even when they don't mean to eavesdrop. I heard snippets about "the weasel" and Jimmy Fratianno, one of Dad's poker buddies. Something about being owed something. The voices all sounded terse, annoyed. There was another word—I couldn't quite get it—Mom muttered it under her breath when she didn't think I was around. *Mafia*? To me they were all just Dad's business friends. I wanted to ask Dad what the word meant, but he was spending more and more time away from the house. A lot of stuff to do at work, he said, when I asked why.

I was glad when Mom changed our home phone number. She seemed to breathe easier. I went to the piano and plunked out a song about the new numbers: *seven five eight* . . . I sang my song quietly. Mom looked around the edge of the kitchen at me and shook her head no. I didn't understand why everything had to be so serious all the time. I went into my bedroom, clicked in a cassette tape, and put my headphones on.

God protected my life when I was born, and continued to protect me from danger throughout my childhood. What I didn't realize, as I was gathering both physical bruises and emotional ones, was that God was present with me, guarding my life, and even calling me to Himself. Yet because I didn't yet know how to trust God with the difficult parts of my life, I found ways to escape what felt too painful to face.

That was when I started dancing—not just to the music, but dancing to find happiness. I would replay that scene of withdrawal, of seeking refuge in a medium that soothed, in many different ways, for years to come. Even as a child, an ache had begun to gather in my soul. Something that should have been steady and unswerving was not there. The pain became so unsettling there were times I thought I'd break apart.

Chapter 3

ANGELS WATCHING OVER ME

Most Saturdays during my childhood summers, my dad would be on the Sacramento River, racing his boat with the Capital City Ski and Drag Boat Association. One Saturday when he wasn't racing, my whole family headed out on the boat for a day on the river.

Around eleven o'clock, dad dropped my mom and Tim and me on a small wooded island that about a dozen other people were already enjoying. I was eight and Tim was ten. Making a human chain, we unloaded blankets, towels, coolers, a plastic jug of icy cold lemonade, our family's red umbrella, and plastic pails and shovels. Our task—and by "our task," I definitely mean *my mom's* task—was to start setting up blankets and umbrellas. After unloading all the gear, my dad and Larry, who was eighteen, returned to shore to pick up his friends—who hadn't fit into the boat on the first trip—to join us for the day.

The edge of the island was a steep drop into the water, rather than a gradual shore. So as my mom spread out blankets, anchoring them with jugs and coolers and shoes, I was playing near the water. Wearing my faded red Speedo, I was swinging my arms, and then jumping out into the water as far as my legs would send me. Then I'd climb out of the river and do it again. I was a strong swimmer and felt very comfortable around the water.

I'd sprung into the river about half a dozen times when I jumped so far into the water that the current caught me and began dragging me away from shore. To make matters worse, an undertow was also pulling me beneath the surface.

At first I wrestled against the current. Worried that my mom would fuss at me for "swimming" out too far, I scrambled to paddle back to shore. But in moments I was fighting to keep my head above water.

Tim, who'd started building a sand mountain, was the first to notice.

"Mom!" he shouted, "Lisa's in trouble!"

My mom turned toward the water to see me being yanked away by the current. A non-swimmer for most of her life, she had recently begun attending swim classes at the Cabana Club, but she'd only learned how to tread water. And because we'd left the lifejackets in the ski boat for the next group of passengers, she couldn't even throw me something to help me float.

Frantically scanning the area, she began yelling to the others on the island, "Help! Somebody help me!"

Knowing she couldn't help, Tim bolted toward the river and jumped in. Getting swept up in the same current that had taken me, he reached me quickly. Desperate for rescue, I grabbed onto him and began pulling him under with me.

My mom continued to scream, "Help! My children are drowning!"

Though everyone on the island was watching our drama unfold, not one of them moved a muscle to help.

I'd been pulled underwater twice, and could feel myself being dragged under for a third time. Tim, who was now also trying to keep his head above water, was struggling for air.

Like a wild mama bear whose cubs are at risk, my mother ran downstream to get closer to us, and jumped in the water. Avoiding the powerful current that had caught us, she was pulled out to a spot with a still pool of water, where she furiously treaded water in order to keep her eye on us.

Tim was struggling like I was. My mom wasn't able to reach us. My dad and Larry hadn't returned. And no one on the beach was even standing, let alone coming to help. To this day, I still can't imagine why. Maybe they thought we were playing? Maybe each one thought another would jump in to help? Maybe they thought it wasn't that serious? Or maybe they just didn't want to get involved. I began to imagine drowning as they all watched silently. By this time I knew I wasn't going to get in trouble, but I wasn't convinced I'd live to see my dad return.

What surprised me most about the trauma was that when I truly believed I might die, I wasn't afraid. Having accepted the Lord's salvation a few years earlier, I knew that I'd be with Him. In the most terrifying moments of my life, I experienced an absurd calm, knowing that my life was in God's hands. Exhausted, I kept doing the only thing I knew how to do, which was kicking with my legs and paddling with my arms.

When I was being dragged under for the third time, someone finally intervened. A pair of strong arms reached down for me and lifted me to the surface. Then this rescuer swam to shore and laid me down on the sand. As I was violently hacking and coughing, choking up water, I noticed this unidentified helper returning to the river, with one other helper, to retrieve my brother, and then my mom.

By the time the three of us were able to sit up and speak, the other people on the island had gathered around us, just as my dad and the teenagers were pulling up to shore.

Pushing through the crowd, my dad demanded to know what was going on. My mom and Tim and I all started blurting out our stories at once. I could read my dad's face to see that he was angry and scared.

When we got to the end of our story, everyone began looking around for the men who'd rescued us. Not only were they nowhere to be seen, but no one onshore had seen them arrive on the island or leave it. Everyone gathered agreed that two strong men had pulled us out of the water and placed us on shore, but it was as if they had disappeared into thin air. Someone in the crowd suggested they may have been lifeguards from Folsom Lake, but that was thirty miles away. And why would they have ferried all the way out to a tiny island with a handful of visitors? Nothing about it added up. My mom, a mighty woman of faith, believed that we had been rescued by angels. In my memory, they were *huge.*

As we've retold this story at family gatherings throughout the decades, I've often thought of the ways my mother's faith fed my own faith as a child and nourished it over the years. It would have been easy for her to reason away the life-saving wonder that happened that day. She could have explained away miraculous intervention by suggesting something more believable—generous passing boaters, or a strong current thrusting us to shore—that would have made more sense. And for which we could even thank God! But there has never been a question in her mind, or mine, that our lives were saved that day by God's angels who were sent to rescue us.

Throughout our lives, we are invited to *choose* to encounter God. We do that when we honor the moments when God has met us, spoken to us, and rescued us. Over the course of our lives, those moments become the anchors for our faith. The temptation over time, of course, is to minimize what God has done in our lives. We do that when we minimize receiving Jesus Christ during our childhoods. We doubt God's salvation could be effective since we made the decision when we were "just a child." Or we rationalize away seeing God miraculously heal someone we loved, later reasoning that they must have gotten well for some other reason. We dismiss God's goodness when we decide that what was clearly His calling on our lives was nothing more than our own hopes or dreams.

My faith in God is richer today because I choose to recognize and honor those inexplicable moments when God has been faithful to meet me. That Saturday at the river was one of the first ones I remember. And since then I have recognized God's gracious presence and intervention when I needed Him most.

Maybe you've been rescued in a way you knew could only be God's handiwork.

Did an unseen force cause your car to swerve away from danger?

Did you receive what you needed at just the right time?

Were the doctors surprised by an unexpected healing?

Beloved friend, I encourage you to recount and claim the ways that God has met you. Even when your eyes can't see it, even when there's no physical evidence of God's presence, He is with you. The One Who said, "I will never leave you or forsake you" can be taken at His word. When your father is across the river, when your mother is stuck treading water, when your brother is fighting for his own life, God can rescue you.

The One Who is all-powerful has your life in His strong arms.

Chapter 4

DEVASTATED

I was all set to dive from the three-meter board at the club when Susan Taylor's taunt caught me cold.

"Hey Lisa!" she yelled across the pool. "I heard your parents are getting a divorce!"

She stood in the shallow end near the silver ladders that led up from the pool, her hands on her hips.

"No they're not," I yelled back.

In a few seconds my mind did a panicked inventory of my home life. If my parents were getting a divorce, I certainly hadn't heard anything about it. Susan was the girl I had stolen the swimsuit from. I don't think she had ever forgiven me for it. We were in the same fifth-grade class at school. Just the day before she had paused by my desk near the pencil sharpener and announced that my dress was the ugliest thing she had ever seen. My mom always dressed me well, in little knits. I knew my dress wasn't ugly. It was just Susan's mean streak. Surely it was that again, rearing up at the pool.

"Yeah they are," Susan said. "Your folks are splitting up. My mom read *all about it* in the newspaper." There was something about the way she accentuated "all about it" that made me wonder if Susan was actually telling the truth. But how could that be? Dad wasn't home a lot, but whenever he was around, he was always hugging Mom. I could still picture him: just a week earlier when he'd been home from a business trip, he had come up behind Mom in the kitchen, wrapped his arms around her, and held her in a long hug. That sort of thing was always happening in our house. Wasn't it? I could feel all the kids in the pool looking at me. My face was burning. It wasn't from the afternoon sun.

It was just a bunch of us kids splashing around at the club that day. It wasn't a practice or a swim team meet. There weren't any adults around except a college-aged lifeguard with a whistle around his neck somewhere near the lap pool. I had climbed to the three-meter board intending to do a forward one-and-a-half, my favorite dive, and one I practiced incessantly, even on my own time. My coach worried that I obsessed about my form, but to me, every dive had to be faultless. It didn't matter what I undertook—music, swimming, friendships—I was already sowing the nervous seeds of perfectionism. But after Susan Taylor's comment, this was one dive that suddenly turned unimportant compared with finding out the truth.

I took a deep breath and dove out as far as I could. Splashing into the water, I swam underneath the surface, ducking under the buoyed nylon rope bordering the deep end, tightening my chest, holding back my tears, hiding underwater from the stares above. I swam and I swam, farther than I had ever gone underwater before, feeling the pressure grow and hammer at my head and lungs and heart. When my fingers brushed the cement edge near the steps at the far shallow end of the pool I hauled myself up, struggling for air. I walked straight-faced into the girls' changing room and put on my clothes over my wet swimsuit. My pants soaked through against the banana seat of my Schwinn as I peddled home, the afternoon air strangely cold for Sacramento in the late spring.

"Mom!" I yelled as I leaned my bike up against the side of the house. There was no answer. "Mom!" Our front door was locked. "Mom!"

I fumbled for the key we kept under the mat. The big house was empty. There was the same linoleum floor and counter, sand colored, the same white-and-gold velour crushed divans, the same solid slab marble coffee table, cream colored. But everything was different. I could hear the mantle clock ticking in the silence. It wasn't like Mom to be gone and not leave a note. I was all alone.

My brother, Larry, eighteen, had already moved out. Just Tim and I were left in the house. Larry was partying hard by then, playing electric guitar in a rock band—a few bands actually: The Intruders, The Working Class, The Psy-Kicks—all the girls at school knew the names of bands that Larry was in. Once at school an older girl had grabbed the handlebars of my bike and wouldn't let go until I promised I'd tell my brother I'd seen her and that she'd said "hello." It was scary. I wished Larry was home right now. He'd know what to do. But he and Dad were constantly fighting before Larry moved out. Dad was a businessman. There was a bottom line to all his career moves. Being in a band was stupid, he said. "Musicians never get anywhere in life."

Tim would be home soon. He was probably just over at a friend's house. Mom was working, I guessed, or helping out at one of Dad's restaurants, or maybe out shopping. I went to the kitchen and fixed myself a BLT for dinner, vigilant to spread mayo all over the bread the way I liked it, careful to cook the bacon crisp but not overdone. When it was all assembled, I cut the sandwich in two. My cut was precise, exactly on the mark. With my world falling into craziness, I was scrambling to find order wherever I could.

Seven o'clock came and went. I sat in front of the TV watching *The Brady Bunch*. Eight o'clock came. I flipped to *Charlie's Angels*. At about nine Tim came home. He didn't say much, just shuffled to his room. He wasn't smiling. Usually whenever he saw me he'd give me a grin or a playful shove on the arm. He used to wake me up by shoving a stinky sock in my face, saying, "Stinky Winky at your service!" before running away. It was always great fun. But there was no kidding around tonight. At ten o'clock I wrote a note to my mom asking her to please wake me up whenever she got home and tell me what was happening. I crawled under the covers and shut my eyes.

I didn't know what time it was when I felt Mom sitting down on the edge of my bed. She gave me a warm hug and held me for a few minutes. "Go back to sleep," she said. "We'll talk about it in the morning." I rolled over on my back. She lightly rubbed my brow, stroking my cheek, running her fingers down the sides of my hair, which she often did. I could feel her gaze on me in the darkness.

"I'm sorry you found out this way, honey. I'm really sorry," she said.

I think she was still sitting on my bed, lightly scratching my back, when I drifted off to sleep.

* * *

Mom filled us in the next morning—mostly large-scale information. Yes, they had been having some disagreements, yes, a divorce was in the works, and yes, the information was already in the newspaper. It wasn't until years later that we found out the full story. Mom had reached the boiling point. For years she had wondered about other women in Dad's life. There were all sorts of hints: lipstick on his collar, strange phone numbers in female handwriting stuffed in his pockets, late nights when he wasn't where he said he'd be. It was the evening she caught him that actually pushed her over the edge. Mom and Dad had a standing date every Friday at a restaurant named Aldo's. They even had their own booth. It was one of her favorite routines. She'd go get her hair done, then meet Dad for their lunch date. One night when he was supposed to be home she went looking for him. She found him at Aldo's—only this time it was a leggy brunette next to him.

Mom walked up behind Dad, placed her hand on his shoulder, and calmly asked him, "Don't you think it's time to come home?"

Startled, his face turned pale and he stood immediately to leave with Mom.

Mom apologized for not telling us about the divorce sooner. She was waiting for the right time, but I guess Susan Taylor picked the time for us. Dad had his own apartment within a couple of weeks. I never confronted him about the divorce or the affairs; we didn't have the type of relationship where we could talk freely. Mom drove us to Dad's apartment for visitation. We'd go there for Friday and Saturday nights, then Dad would bring us home on Sunday afternoons. We were supposed to go there every other weekend, but soon it turned into once a month; sometimes six weeks went by between visitations. There was one spare room in Dad's apartment; sometimes Tim would take it and I'd have the couch in the living room. Other times we'd reverse. Sometimes Dad had other people sleeping over in the apartment, and Tim and I would both sleep on the floor.

When your parents get divorced, your foundation crumbles, whatever foundation you thought you had. I always believed my family was secure. Even when Dad wasn't around for long periods of time, I had convinced myself that things were normal that way, even when we went on vacations without him, even when he wasn't at home night after night, I convinced myself that Dad's love was always there, always within reach. I held to this hope tightly. One time when I was in Bluebirds, a junior Campfire Girls program, we had a daddy-daughter dinner at school, and Dad took me. I'd been anticipating the night for weeks, and was so proud of my carefully coiffed hairstyle and to be wearing a new dress and new shoes. He looked so handsome in his new olive green silk suit. I felt so proud to be with him. But all the way through dinner he kept looking at his watch—like there was somewhere else he had to be. Or wanted to be. I kept eating my chicken, the rip inside me gaining new ground. I always wanted to be special to him. I wanted him to love me. I desperately wanted to believe that he did love me. At least when Mom and Dad were together, I could pretend that Dad's love was within reach. After the divorce, I was sure about one thing—Dad didn't want us around. He never would have had his affairs if he did.

Even on weekends when Tim and I were over at Dad's apartment he wasn't around much, but we found moments of normalcy at the lake nearby and an old wooden raft. Tim and I would pole around on the raft, pretending we were Tom Sawyer and Huck Finn. Dad would always be at work. Or somewhere. A year or two after the divorce Dad took us on a trip to Aspen. He bought me a new ski jacket. The trip was going to be perfect. But Dad's new girlfriend just "happened" to show up right where we were. She ruined everything. She had a movie star figure and long dark hair, worn up in a bun. When she hugged me her huge chest felt knobby and hard—I'm sure she had silicone implants. Dad married her soon after that trip. She tried to be kind to me. Once she bought me a tangerine polka dotted bikini to wear at Dad's pool. It was the nicest thing she did. The marriage lasted a year, then they had it annulled.

My best comfort continued to be found in music. Mom saw how much I loved music and how much it moved me. I was already playing the piano constantly, so she talked to Jory Waldon, our church's music pastor, and signed me up for voice lessons with him. Pastor Jory was gentle, soft-spoken, and sensitive. He was middle-aged, tall with dark hair. He taught me the value of notes and how to sing from my diaphragm. Lessons were held after school once a week. I took them for about six months. Those voice lessons with Jory Waldon were the one bright spot in that season of my life. Once a week I got to think about something else besides the pain I felt inside me.

Life continues after a divorce. Month follows month, and year follows year. At first, my parents' divorce renewed my resolve to be perfect. Any time I saw my dad I'd go to great lengths to win his approval. I got perfect grades in the latter years of elementary school and first years of junior high. I excelled on the swim team. I was flawless at music. I was the perfect daughter for my father, or so I hoped. Maybe that would work. Once I grew my nails out long and painted them an unblemished pink.

"Look Dad, what do you think?" I said, spreading out my fingers to display the nails to him.

He said, "What are they—fake?" as he pulled on them.

His comment crushed me. I knew it shouldn't have, but I had done it specifically to win his approval. I was an easy target to any offhanded remark devastating me. I was fragile beyond words.

* * *

While, at the time, I still believed I'd had a somewhat idyllic American childhood, it didn't take a degree in counseling to notice the throbbing hurts I carried in my heart. Like every little girl, I longed for the loving gaze and ear and presence of my father. But his attention was divided. Business, alcohol, gambling, and other women had all kept him distracted from what ought to have mattered most. I had no idea what to do with the feelings that were buried deep in my heart.

Maybe the hurts you carry in your heart are similar to mine and maybe they're different. Maybe you lived in a home with violence that was directed toward you or others. Maybe you lost a parent to death or abandonment. Maybe there was someone else who wasn't a safe person when you were young. Beloved, those earliest hurts matter to God, who longs to heal and redeem. God sees your pain and God hears your cry. But perhaps, like me, you've self-soothed and self-medicated over the years.

We all manage our pain in different ways, and one of my go-to strategies was working to be so perfect that my dad *and everyone else* would have to love me. Trying to be perfect tends to tire you out before long. Although I doubt if I articulated it, I know my subconscious was busy trying to find another way to deal with my pain.

Chapter 5

QUEEN ILENE

The day I learned of my parents' divorce and fell asleep with my mother gently scratching my back, is an apt—if incomplete—snapshot of the woman I knew during my childhood. She corralled her own pain to tend to mine. As is true of most children and their mothers, what I knew of Ilene Daggs was contingent on all the ways she related to me and cared for me. In time, though, I would discover who she was to others.

And that someone was pretty amazing.

Just prior to the Great Depression, Ilene Verle was born into the Dawson family in Aledo, Illinois. Like many in their farming community, their daily life was impacted by poverty. The youngest of five children, Ilene Verle was preceded by her twin sister Irene Merle by minutes. When her father would pour himself a drink each night, his children would run to him with their empty tin cups, begging for whatever he was consuming, before he swatted them away. But one evening he obliged my mother, who was just three years old; halfway through the meal she fell over backward onto the floor, drunk! A harsh man, Elmer Dawson would line up all five children when one committed an infraction and give each a beating.

But despite her harsh upbringing, my mother grew up to become a rare gem who radiated outer beauty from a soul that was full of love for others.

As spunky as she was radiant, at sixteen she left Illinois to make her way to Los Angeles, where she began waitressing at a restaurant called Harper's Night Owl, a popular dive for military men. A striking blonde beauty, she caught the eye of many customers, who she also won over with her warm personality. Ilene met a soldier and was soon engaged.

Her fiancé was serving in Europe during World War II when Robert Austin Daggs walked into the Night Owl.

Spotting him from across the room, leaning over to her friend Gracie, Ilene announced, "I'm gonna marry that man!"

There wasn't much chance that Bob Daggs was not going to notice her. A rare charm welled up from her soul that attracted anyone she met, and Bob Daggs was smitten. After Ilene sent a "Dear John" letter to break off her engagement to the soldier, she and Bob became an item. They were both amazing dancers, and when they'd go out dancing on her nights away from the restaurant, the floor would clear as they jitterbugged the night away.

As foretold, Ilene's love-at-first-sight announcement came to pass. Within a year of marrying my father, they welcomed my oldest brother, Larry Steven Daggs.

A few years later, when Larry was at preschool, my mother was straightening the house when the doorbell rang. She opened it to find a middle-aged woman carrying a Bible almost as big as a toddler. She introduced herself as Mama Wold, a Four-Square missionary. Filled with God's love, she'd come to share the Gospel with anyone in that little Los Angeles neighborhood who would receive it. My mother lapped up every word that fell from her lips, receiving Christ as her savior before Mama Wold left the porch.

After that first visit, the two continued to meet regularly, and Ilene continued to fall head over heels in love with Jesus. Careful to balance the demands of her new marriage and her infant son, my mother began attending church and participating in street ministry outreach in downtown Los Angeles. With no small amount of prodding, my dad would join her in the pew each Sunday morning.

Eight years after Larry was born, my parents welcomed my brother Tim, and sixteen months later they completed their family with me.

When I was three my parents purchased the house in Sacramento where my mother lived the rest of her days. While she cared for us children, my father launched six Smorgy Boys restaurants.

Because my most pressing childhood concerns revolved around which friends would be at the Cabana Club each day, and because there wasn't any observable discord at home, I was in the dark about my parents' increasingly troubled marriage. I was oblivious to the reasons for my father's frequent absences from the home, and never wondered why my mom would leave his dinner warming in the oven while we attended evening activities at church. I didn't understand the way booze affected him and our family. I didn't know about his gambling habit. I certainly never imagined him spending time with any woman other than my mother.

So when I heard the news about my parents' impending divorce at the top of the three-meter board at the club that day, the foundation on which my world had been built suddenly shifted. My father moved seventy-five miles west to Concord, California, while my mother stayed in our home and cared for us, depending on dad's monthly checks. My biweekly weekend visits with Tim to Dad's new apartment became less frequent. So did the support checks. When she had no choice but to find a job, my mom did some catering with a friend from church and eventually worked long, hard hours as a hostess at a steak house, where her people skills shined.

My mother's true passion, in addition to her children, was sharing Jesus's love with others. Beyond her active involvement in our church, she opened the doors of our home every Friday night to whoever would come. When she'd meet teens and young adults in the community, at the grocery store or walking down the street, she'd invite them join and learn more about Jesus. When one of these newcomers would knock tentatively on our door, she'd greet him or her with a kiss and warm embrace. On most Fridays, there would be anywhere from thirty to sixty young people packed into our home. From football players to misfits, my mother made everyone feel special and loved. When any of them had needs, she'd step up to care for them, taking one to JC Penney's for an outfit or two to interview for a job, or taking another to the hairdresser or barber shop for a trim. When they gave their lives to the Lord, she even baptized some of them in our bathtub!

One of her greatest joys was to pray with those who were hurting. My mom invited countless suffering souls into our home, where she'd lead them to a corner in the living room with two cushy chairs. Once settled there, heartbroken individuals would tell her the stories of their lives, and then, in the presence of Jesus, Mama would lead them through a prayer process called "healing of the memories." And because she was such a holy secret-keeper, I never once was privy to the details of anyone else's story. She was both trustworthy and loyal, without a hint of judgment.

My mother's ministry of healing was both spiritual and physical. Whenever she learned that someone was sick, she'd make them a pot of chicken soup, boiling the chicken until the meat fell away from the bone, because the healing, she said, was in the marrow. As I'd hustle through the kitchen on my way to watch TV or walk to a friend's house, I saw her make hundreds of pots of chicken soup over the years. Two pastors, both near death, credit their recovery to the power of both Queen Ilene's chicken soup and prayers. To the devil's dismay, her chicken-soup-and-prayer combo was formidable! What I wouldn't find out until years later (from others, not my mom) was how she struggled financially. And yet her robust generosity never waned.

Every morning I'd see her at the kitchen table, where she'd already been devouring God's Word for several hours. Through the years she went through Bible after Bible, each one eventually suffering from broken bindings and loose pages from being used so much. When the Lord prompted her to share a word with someone, she never shied away from it. Though countless people who met her experienced her as the warmest, most gracious, affectionate woman, she was bold and strong with God's Word when He gave her an assignment.

The day Jesus got a hold of Ilene Daggs on the front steps of her home, the Kingdom gained a mighty warrior.

It's impossible to quantify how many were touched and transformed by my mother's beautiful ministry. She knew her purpose and was passionate about fulfilling it. She just oozed God's love to family, to acquaintances, and to strangers. Every Friday, she'd visit the Olive Tree beauty shop, and instead of closing her eyes and relaxing, she would try to win her stylist, Joyce, to the Lord!

You know how savvy businesspeople are always ready with a professional-looking business card, prepared to advance their careers at a moment's notice if they meet someone who can do something for them? My mother had her own business cards printed, and she was never without them. They said:

If you meet me and forget me, you've lost nothing.
If you meet Jesus, and forget Him, you've lost everything.
Need prayer? Call Ilene.

She included our phone number, and I would often see her in the kitchen or living room, eyes closed in prayer, with the receiver pressed to her ear at the end of a long, twisty cord, listening to someone she'd met at the Olive Tree or at the grocery store spill out their hearts.

Over the years, friends and strangers who received one of those little business cards have shared with me testimonies of who Ilene Daggs was to them. One woman reported that after her mother died, my mom rushed to her home, curlers still in her hair, to offer love and support. Another woman, who lived in my mother's home with her son when they would have been homeless, raved, "I had no idea that God was going to show me in skin and bones what it was like to live with a person totally surrendered and submitted to her Lord and Savior Jesus Christ." And yet another woman my mom invited to church testified that she heard God speak audibly to her during prayer in worship. Though my mother was right beside her, she heard no audible words. And yet when the guest told her about the miracle on the way home, my mom, who'd heard *in her spirit* exactly what the Lord had spoken to the woman, flashed her gorgeous smile and said simply, "I know."

The rare and precious commodity she offered so many was radically unconditional love. If you've never received it, I so wish you could see it radiating from her tiny frame. Being fully welcomed, without the smallest hint of judgment, is a gift Ilene Daggs gave to everyone she met. Through her deeds, she delivered God's presence to many in ways that even the best words from preachers or teachers never could.

Though I was slow to grasp it as a girl, and often resented the amount of energy she spent on others, there is no question in my mind that my life could have turned out very differently without her fierce, prayerful protection and guidance. I will be forever grateful to my Savior for picking Queen Ilene to be my mama. In time I would even come not only to accept, but to celebrate, that she wasn't just the best mom to me, but to countless others.

As I prepared to enter adolescence, I had no idea how much I would need her.

Chapter 6

PARTY GIRL

If I'd mostly stayed on the straight and narrow for the first twelve
years of my life, middle school was the season when my path got
a little . . . less narrow.

Debbie lived about a half mile from me. We could ride our bikes
to each other's houses. Across the street from Debbie lived another
friend, Julie. Around the corner lived Cindy. Barbara lived in Rosemont, near my house. By tenth grade, the five of us had become
inseparable.

Only Julie had any sort of question mark over her reputation. The
rest of us were all good kids. It wasn't like we made a conscious decision to be wild. Maybe our first steps that direction were just for fun.
We knew experimenting with wildness was not something we were
supposed to do, so it felt daring. We felt grown up. We could not yet
see any consequence.

At a sleepover at Debbie's the five of us broke into her parents'
liquor cabinet. They were out for the evening, and we passed around
gin, vodka, whiskey, and tequila, tasting the harsh-bitter flavors,
feeling for the first time the wonderfully numbing effect of too
much booze. My mom had once given me a bit of wine for men-
strual cramps, and I'd loved the taste of it—the warmth immediately

on the back of my tongue, the way it flowered a little and slid all the way down my throat. Little did I know that it was a snake about to bite.

The next week, my friends and I drank together again. There was a 7-Eleven on the corner of Folsom Boulevard and La Riviera Drive, right at the entrance to Larchmont, the neighborhood where Debbie lived. We hung out at the 7-Eleven that evening, asking people if they'd buy a bottle for us. *No, we're not fourteen. We're in college. We've left our IDs back at the dorm.* Nobody was that stupid. But one guy bought a bottle for us anyway. He wanted to be invited along wherever the party was. We gave him our money, then scampered away. This party was just for us girls.

We headed down to the levy by the American River, two bottles of Boones Farm apple wine in tow. Before the levy was a huge grassy field. We stayed in the field drinking our wine, laughing, giddy, forgetting the world around us as the alcohol poured into our pubescent bloodstreams.

Down by the river was where the real party was taking place. We all knew it. We had heard about it at school. Part of a great big tree had busted off and stuck in the water. The site was nicknamed The Log. All the really cool high school campfires and keggers were held there. Parties at The Log were a regular occurrence. But that wasn't what we were all about. Was it?

We told ourselves our lines in the sand were firm. But in a few weeks we were joining other parties, and other people were joining ours—my brother and his friends, high school guys, guys we didn't know. The mix of older guys and younger girls made everything get messy. Soon it all blurred together. At first we went to The Log only a couple times a month. Then it was a party most weekends. Before long, it was every day after school.

But it was a headachy, throbbing, vomiting kind of fun that we chased. And we sensed that the friends who thought we were cool (we hoped) were just as insecure as we were. And whatever pain we thought we were drowning the night before was still there the next morning, only worse.

Day after day when I woke up, I knew that much was true.

* * *

We also had friends who were eager to sell us weed. When my mom found some in my pocket in tenth grade, I earnestly said what every teenager everywhere says when their mother finds an illicit substance in their possession: "It's not mine. I'm holding it for a friend."

Yeah, I thought I was pretty clever.

My mom wasn't buying it. She told the school counselor, which meant I got called in and had to listen to grave warnings about the kinds of choices I was making. I purposed to look humble and remorseful, but I had no intention of making better choices.

In January of my freshman year of high school, my brother Tim and I were heading to Tower Records in the new cherry-red Austin Healy Sprite my dad had given him for his sixteenth birthday. Rain plunked down on the windshield, and four of our friends followed behind us in a pale blue Chevy Impala.

Tim was cruising down Watt Avenue, toward the intersection at Fair Oaks Boulevard. Because we had a green light, he didn't slow down. Who would? What neither one of us noticed was an old man with his blinker on in the center lane, who was driving a three-quarter ton truck. When Tim finally saw the obstacle ahead of us, he hit the brakes, skidding forward with tires squealing, barely avoiding rear-ending the truck. But my head still smacked the windshield.

Unfortunately, our friends in the Impala were even less focused on the road than we'd been. In fact, while Ron was in the back seat rolling a joint, John, who was driving, turned around for a moment to supervise, instructing Ron to remove the seeds. When he turned back toward the road, sailing along at forty miles per hour, there was no time for him to stop before hitting us.

The impact from behind shoved our car into the back of the truck, and my head smacked the windshield a second time. Tim's body was also thrown forward, slamming into the steering wheel and the rearview mirror.

After the second impact, Tim and I were both stunned. Though wildly unlikely, we were both able to open our doors and step out of the car into the street. All of the traffic had come to a standstill, and as I exited the car I felt cool raindrops on my face. The front and back of the car had crumpled, and it was clear it would never be driven again.

Dazed, Tim and I looked at each other with wide-eyed "I can't believe it" faces.

"Are you okay?" he asked.

"I think so," I said. "How about you?"

"I think I'm . . ." Tim began, wanting to reassure me he was fine, but he never finished that sentence.

Shards of glass that had been securely lodged in his cheeks, chin, and forehead came loose when he started talking, and blood began gushing from his face.

When paramedics arrived, we were both transported to Sutter Hospital. A few minutes later, my mom, who'd gotten a phone call from John, met me in the waiting room while Tim got stitched up.

As we were waiting several hours together, I started to notice I was having trouble moving my head. After four hours I was admitted to a room to be examined, and left that day wearing the kind of spongy white foam neck braces I'd seen on television, most often when someone was faking being injured in a car accident! I wish I'd been faking, but the pain was real. I was also sentenced to physical therapy, which included being put into traction. Nurses would lay hot packs on me, and then I would be strapped into a traction machine that would stretch me from hips to head, then release. Stretch and release. I had to endure the process three times a week for over a month.

While some teenagers might have learned from the cautionary tale, and chosen to avoid drugs I was not one of them.

The summer after my first year of high school, my friends and I would buy sweet cherry popsicles from the snack bar at the Cabana Club, work on our tans, and titter about boys. And in my case, that meant Gary. Gary had a two-tone gray Corvette, the kind with a long "U" on the side. Although my mom thought he was a great kid, she didn't want me spending a lot of time with him.

I was fifteen; Gary was twenty.

And the flirting was *on*.

On my sixteenth birthday, my friends and I bought three joints. For an investment of eleven dollars, we got two that were three dollars each, and a fancy one that was five dollars. Because it was my birthday, my brother Tim and his friends encouraged me to take a big hit of the "special" one, holding the smoke in my mouth and lungs. It didn't take me long to realize that what made that one so special was that it was laced with PCP.

When I moved, I felt like I was walking on air. Though I could see my feet touching the grassy hill near the levy, it felt like I was walking four feet off the ground. As I meandered aimlessly, to the amusement of my audience, I realized I'd had too much.

Lying down in the grass near the river, close to passing out, my half-sleeping, half-waking mind cycled through absurd dreams. Sick to my stomach, I felt like I was dying. In this absurd alternate universe, I do have a very clear memory of reading a newspaper headline that announced, "Sixteen-Year-Old Dies On Her Birthday."

At the moment, it felt like a very strong possibility.

When I would come to for a moment, I begged my mind to focus. Despite the haze from tripping, I was aware that my family had plans that evening to celebrate my Sweet Sixteen. I knew I had to find a way to stumble home, because my mom was excited to take us all to a Polynesian restaurant called The Coral Reef that served the most amazing deep-fried prawns, chow mein, and foil-wrapped chicken. The exclusive guest list for the special night included my mom, Tim, my friend Barbara, and me.

Against all odds, I made it home, changed out of my Levis bell bottoms and into a cute dress, forced a smile, and we all went out to dinner. Seeing some of my favorite foods, I felt nauseous, and I probably looked it.

Although she didn't accuse, scold, or explode, my savvy mom knew *something* was wrong.

Not long after my birthday, Gary and I got . . . closer. My mom, who still had two kids at home to support, would often work late at the restaurant. And when the cat was away, Gary and I would play. One night she came home earlier than I'd expected. When we heard the front door swing open, we both panicked. Because the first thing she did after work was set eyes on Tim and me to ask about our days, I knew she'd be headed for my room. Frantic, hearing her tired footsteps in the wooden hallway, I shoved Gary into my closet, and then sprawled across my bed to give the impression I'd been reading.

Opening the door of my room, my mom calmly announced, "Gary, come out of the closet. You can go home now."

Moms just *know.*

As I began partying more with my friends when I was sixteen and seventeen, I grew away from Gary. A lot of nights, after my mom would check in on me, I'd sneak out my window and meet my girls, riding our bikes to the Glenbrook neighborhood to hang out with friends who lived there. Or we'd all hop in my car and cruise through the neighborhoods. When we were low on gas, Julie would siphon some out of big motorhomes parked beside people's houses.

Basically, during my adolescence, I decided that I was the boss of me. And while none of the choices I was making seemed like a very big deal at the time—or at least I convinced myself that they weren't— each one took me another step further from being the girl and young woman I'd been created to be.

That's the way it happens for all of us, isn't it?

While your choices may not be the kinds of illegal, mind-altering ones I was making, the daily decisions we make about how to live our lives—what to eat, what to buy, what media to consume, who to date, and more—are what shape us. When we stubbornly choose our own way, we numb ourselves to what our choices are doing to us.

And then one day we wake up, look around, and ask, "How did I get here?"

I know how I got there and I know how you got there: one choice at a time. When I was a teen, I assumed the extent of the consequences of my sin were hangovers, headaches, and pools of vomit.

They weren't.

Graciously, in addition to the natural consequences for our choices, there is also God's plentiful merciful grace. For me. For you.

Chapter 1

MY DREAM—AND I DO MEAN *Mine*

Despite all the partying I'd done in high school, I managed to serve as captain on the cheer team and even succeeded academically. But when I pictured my future, I didn't see college, grad school, or success in the business world. If I closed my eyes and imagined my dream future, I saw myself on a stage, singing my heart out, being lauded by adoring fans. Yes, it would be great to be adored by millions, but there was also something deeper going on in my heart. Although I didn't have the words to name it at the time, when I sang I was being the person I was made to be. I felt alive in a way nothing else made me feel. I knew it was what I was born to do, and I was passionate about realizing my dream.

Not long after I graduated from high school, I entered the Dodge Wrangler Country Showdown, an annual talent contest begun in the early 1980s to discover country music singers. Contestants who went on to make it big included Billy Ray Cyrus, Garth Brooks, and Martina McBride. The regional competition I entered was hosted in Sacramento, and I sang Linda Ronstadt's "Blue Bayou." When

I was named Female Vocalist of Northern California, I felt certain I was on the fast track to stardom.

What actually happened was that I moved to Lake Tahoe, about a hundred miles from where I was raised, to perform and work. If you imagine all the Hollywood hopefuls who are working as baristas and waitresses in Los Angeles, my life was kind of the Northern California version of that. But since I wasn't yet twenty-one, and not allowed to waitress in establishments that served alcohol, I bussed tables at Sahara Casino while trying to book gigs. Pretty glamorous, I know.

In the meantime, I started getting into hash. Made from the resin of the cannabis plant—the same one that produces marijuana—the drug is most often smoked in a pipe. When I had the money, I'd buy hash called Lebanese Blonde, packaged like a brick in cheesecloth. Each brick, army green on the outside and yellow on the inside, was officially stamped as coming from Lebanon. I also bought Thai sticks, which were potent buds with red hairs and THC crystals on them. Tied to a little stick, wound with cat gut string, each stick sold for twenty bucks. While pricy, you didn't need as much of the potent drug to get high. One hit, and you were done.

While I believed I functioned pretty well on drugs, not everyone would agree. One day I showed up at work loaded. My responsibilities included carrying coffee pots on trays, and when I struggled to carry a tray that would have been manageable had I been sober, I came inches from scalding a customer with a hot pot of coffee when it all cascaded onto the casino's dingy red carpet.

Cobbling together an array of part-time jobs, I worked at Nordica Ski Company, a restaurant atop Squaw Valley Mountain Ski Resort, and in the summer I worked at Base Camp as a lifeguard.

At Squaw, I lived in an A-frame cabin with my friend Rosie, who was also from Sacramento. Rosie and I had never done acid, but one evening we met a guy who was working on the tram and selling it at the ski resort, and he promised to hook us up. The next day was working at the bottom of the tram, so we bought the LSD and hopped onboard.

"Terry" had sold us a drug called Mr. Natural, and we bought three hits—three pieces of absorbent paper soaked with the drug that had pictures of a long-haired naked man on them. (Maybe a hippie from Woodstock?) So, as the tram began its ascent, we each swallowed the papers. Unfortunately, that meant that Mr. Natural started to kick in as we were still on the tram. Panicked, we coached each other to be cool until we got back to Rosie's car at the bottom of the mountain.

Rosie was supposed to renew her license in a nearby town called Truckee that day, but, laughing hysterically, she realized she was in no condition to be interacting with government officials. Though we both should have had the good sense to keep her from driving, neither one of us did. So we drove from Squaw to Truckee to Alpine Meadows to River Ranch to the North Shore, and then repeated the same loop for hours, listening to Bob Seger and the Silver Bullet Band singing "Hollywood Nights" for most of them. When I finally got home some ten hours later, in a dirty yellow-and-white striped T-shirt, once-white tennis shorts now a dingy brown, and with dirt under my broken fingernails, I knew I never wanted to feel that out of control again.

Most likely because of all the partying, and very little good nutrition to balance all the junk I was putting in my body, I caught the Russian flu. Very quickly, I was unable to function. Two weeks later, when my mom came to pick me up to return home to live with her in Sacramento, I was sick. I was tired. I was weary. I knew I'd made a mess of my life.

As if I somehow became a different person with the move, I returned to my home church and started dating a guy there. I was nineteen and Jeff was twenty-four. My mom loved that he was a Christian. I loved that he was a handsome singer. And he owned a house! He had a sound system set up in his living room and we'd take turn singing songs. Our beginnings were pretty sweet. I felt acceptance from him and like I was ready to settle down with a cute, charming, Christian boy who liked to sing. What could go wrong?

Well, other stuff.

Because Jeff had been acting kind of possessive and clingy, I was grateful for a Friday night out with my girlfriends, attending a party at a nearby restaurant. Committed to my new lifestyle, wanting to live differently, I vowed to myself that I wouldn't drink or use. To this day, I don't believe I did drink or use that night, but I do think someone may have slipped something into my soda. I started to feel dizzy and a little woozy about halfway through the evening. A light-skinned, green-eyed guy I worked with, Yaponcha, was kind enough to drive me home after the party.

What neither of us realized was that Jeff had been driving up and down my street, waiting for me to get home.

Yaponcha dropped me off in the driveway and was waiting to make sure I got into my house safely when Jeff parked and marched up to me.

He shouted, "Where have you been?"

Something in his voice scared me. The way he spoke told me that he'd come unhinged.

As Yaponcha tried to back out of the driveway, Jeff confronted him, acting wildly jealous, and even trying to pull him out through the car window.

"Where have you been?" Jeff bellowed again, in my direction.

I half-feared and half-hoped my mother or a neighbor would come out to see what the commotion was.

"I went to a party," I reminded him, keeping my voice calm so as not to upset him further.

Jeff had given me a pair of ruby stud earrings for my birthday, and I was wearing them that evening. Noticing them, he continued to rage.

"I want my earrings back," he demanded.

"But you gave them—" I began to protest. But when I saw the fire in his eyes, I loosened the back of the left earring, pulled out the stud, and dropped it into Jeff's open waiting hand. I watched him put it in his shirt pocket.

By this point, overwhelmed with sadness and still feeling lousy and a little confused, I was blubbering like a baby.

I removed the second earring, but I'd had enough of his bullying. Instead of dutifully dropping it into his hand, I threw it at him. It bounced off his blue flannel shirt and into the grass.

At that point, the look on his face really scared me. Before I realized what was happening, Jeff drew his arm back and punched me in the eye.

I'd been standing on the top step leading to my mom's front door, but because he was so much bigger and stronger than me, I crumpled at the blow, falling toward the front door and to the ground.

After Jeff stormed off, I quietly entered the house, locked the door, and slipped into bed. I was so exhausted I didn't even change into my pajamas, I just crashed on top of my bed.

The next morning my alarm went off as 5:45, when I usually rose to get ready for work. Stumbling to the bathroom, I saw that the area around my eye had swollen up into a blood-blue shiner. There was no hiding the injury, since my left eye was already swollen shut, but I thought I could at least lighten the color. I winced as I tried to put concealer and makeup over it. When I failed to disguise it, I just called in to work sick. I also lied to my mom, saying I'd stumbled into a railing at the party.

When Jeff got off work that afternoon, he came straight to my house. Though I didn't want to see him, my mom, who was none the wiser, let him in and gave us privacy to chat in the living room.

"Baby," he began, "I'm so sorry."

Emboldened from knowing my mother was nearby and still nursing a bruised heart, I stood my ground and refused to forgive him and be reconciled. Over the next few days, though, he was persistent. Eventually I took him back.

One Friday night a bunch of friends from work and I were partying after our shifts at a six-top round table, and I saw Jeff walk in. I'd told him my plans, but I had not invited him.

Smiling politely, he greeted everyone at the table.

Then, quietly, he asked, "Can we talk?"

We'd had a conflict the previous evening, and I really didn't feel like the restaurant was the right place to deal with it. I didn't leave the table, but I gave him an opportunity to say what he wanted to say.

"We can talk here," I offered, pulling my seat back a bit from the rest of the table.

"Can we step outside?" he asked. "I promise I won't hurt you. I just want to talk."

I relented, and agreed to talk outside the restaurant.

"Hey guys," I announced to the group of girl and guy friends at the table, "I'll be right back."

Stepping into the foyer of the restaurant, between the reception desk and the parking lot, Jeff yanked my hand and grabbed me by the hair.

Forcefully, he dragged me across two busy lanes of traffic to the other side of the street, where my car was parked. I struggled to maintain my footing, in high heels, trying to keep up with his fast pace. Though I'd felt somewhat safe near the restaurant where my friends continued to banter, I suddenly felt very vulnerable and very scared.

Eyes darting around the scene for help, I spotted a pair of cops standing by their car at a nearby gas station.

"Help!" I screamed, knowing I might have only one chance before Jeff silenced me.

"HELP!" I hollered again.

The officers, seeing I was being held against my will, ran over and asked Jeff to release me. He acted like nothing was wrong, but the cops had heard the fear in my voice and seen it in my eyes.

Splitting up, one of the officers talked to me and one talked to Jeff. After exchanging accounts with one another, the taller one asked me, "Do you want to press charges?"

What I thought, but didn't say, was that I'd experienced much worse than what just happened to me. Jeff had grown increasingly jealous and controlling, and our "scuffles" had become more frequent and more dangerous.

I couldn't even imagine what kind of time bomb I'd ignite if I pressed charges.

"No," I answered, "But let me get in my car and get a head start. I just want to get home."

Dubious, but compliant, the officers watched as I slid behind the wheel and turned onto the road.

I'd only driven about four blocks when I glanced in the rearview mirror and saw a madman driving behind me. Terrified, remembering how he'd assaulted me in front of my mom's home before, I felt completely vulnerable. Stepping on the gas, I let my instincts take over.

I was half a block from a traffic light already turning from yellow to red.

My window was rolled down about six inches, and as I waited at the light, praying for it to change quickly, Jeff ran from his car to mine, and thrust both hands through the opening.

"Please, please, please, please . . ." I begged the light and the universe, "turn, turn, turn . . .."

The moment the light turned green, I hit the gas.

Like the crazy person he was in that moment, Jeff continued to run alongside my car, hanging on to my window, through the intersection, until he was practically horizontal!

When he couldn't keep up with me, he let go. I continued to drive like a bat out of hell, trying to get home. I even took shortcuts through a few sketchy neighborhoods I'd typically avoid. Confident I had the jump on him, I roared into the driveway, shut off my car, raced inside, and locked the door behind me.

Leaning against the back of the door, breathing a deep sigh of relief, I was grateful to be safe.

Though I made it through that night, Jeff's chaotic behavior continued. One night when he was chasing my car, he flipped his Volkswagen. I waited just long enough to see him emerge from the car, and then sped home. And one Easter morning, after flipping a second car in my mom's neighborhood because of his erratic driving, he terrified me by waking me up at 5:30 a.m., banging on my bedroom window with blood dripping down his face.

As one might imagine, our relationship did not go the distance. Although Jeff and I had been engaged at one point, he found another woman pretty quickly and married her. Less than a year later, he ran his car into a brick wall. My mom actually heard about his accident at church and mentioned it to me. Although it had been a toxic relationship, I felt compelled to visit him in the hospital.

Carefully opening the door, relieved to see no family members, I crept into Jeff's room. He was in a coma, hooked up to all kinds of machines; I knew his brain had swollen and that he was expected to die within a day.

Leaning toward his ear, I whispered, "Jeff, it's Lisa. I forgive you."

Quietly breathing a prayer for mercy, I left the hospital.

As I drove home, I thought about the jarring image of Jeff waiting at death's door, eyes swollen shut, just as he'd done to one of mine.

Although I couldn't see it at the time, when I look back on that season, I believe both that I was at one of several crossroads in my life, and that the Lord was giving me glimpses of the two roads before me. One of them was being traveled by some of the people at our church. I saw them living life that really was life. But God was also giving me glimpses of what that other road looked like. I'd seen the toll that drinking and drugging had taken on friends I'd known at home and in Tahoe. I'd felt the terror of being with someone who would harm me. It was as if the Lord was whispering to my heart, "How much more can you take? How much more are you willing to go through?"

I'd bought the lie of the enemy, hissing in my other ear, "Don't miss out on life! You've gotta have fun. You deserve to have fun! Do what you want to do!"

What I was blind to at that time was that the enemy's road is always death. And each time we fall for it, our hearts harden a little bit.

When I was a girl, my dad had walked out of my life, and there was nothing I could do about it. I'd wanted him so much, and without realizing it, I still needed broken men who I could fix to need *me*. And so I continued to seek wholeness where it would never be found.

Is the Lord whispering to your heart in this season? Is the Spirit inviting you to open your eyes and read the signs in your life? Is that same Spirit convicting you of the part you've played in the messy places in your own life?

If you are ready to see, if you are ready to accept and receive what is most real and most true, invite God to open your eyes. It's what God delights in doing for his children! Ask God to help you identify the ways you're choosing death and to show you what health and wholeness look like. And then have the courage to make the changes, to take the baby steps, that you need to take to live well.

I wish I could say that I was ready to pivot toward the road that leads to life, but I wasn't quite there yet.

Chapter 8

OUT OF CONTROL

While it's hard to imagine this happening today, my mom would pull up in her car next to kids smoking weed and invite them to our home. She'd bait them so that she could tell them about Jesus.

Slowing to a stop, she'd roll down her window and offer, "I want to invite you over Friday night."

Embarrassed, I'd pretend to be looking at something else out the window.

"We have lots of youth," she'd promise, "and plenty of food. It's a great place to meet new friends."

That was always the offer, and—against all odds—kids showed up. Sometimes we'd have fifty or sixty people crammed into our living room for Bible study and prayer.

Dan and his friend Greg were singer/songwriters who also worshiped at Capital Christian Center. They were a bit older, in their early twenties, and like a lot of young people at our church, they trusted my mom for spiritual guidance.

One evening Dan was lounging on our living room sofa when he heard me singing in my bedroom down the hall. When he asked my mom who it was, she proudly announced, "It's my daughter."

She called me into the living room to meet them. I was delighted to have been noticed for my singing. I was continuing to hustle toward realizing my dream, and had been winning local talent contests. When Dan and Greg and I met, we all agreed we should work on something together. Greg was especially gifted at teaching harmonies, and I picked up his lessons quickly. We sang together in churches and camps, but we were hungry for more.

When we finally got into the studio, we made a three-song demo with Cliff "Barney" Robertson, who'd played keys for Waylon Jennings. Dan and I went to Nashville to pitch our demo. When we didn't get signed, we ended up going our separate ways and I kept trying to move forward as a solo act. I returned to Barney's studio and did three more demo songs. And though I kept hustling to book whatever local gigs I could, I wasn't finding the break I'd always dreamed of.

While I wish I could report that attending church and living under my mother's roof helped me stay on the straight and narrow, there was still nothing narrow about the way I was living.

One Saturday night a friend of mine invited me to a Pisces party, celebrating anyone born under the astrological sign straddling February and March. Basically, it was an excuse to party. I'd already had a lot to drink, but as the party wound down I wasn't ready to call it an evening. So I headed to the Oasis Ballroom, a club on 21st Street in Sacramento. They always had a live band, and I knew I'd know people there. As we talked and laughed, I continued to drink.

Stumbling out of the club, I walked a few blocks back to my car—a beautiful gray '52 Plymouth Cranbrook that really was like driving a boat. (In both cases, always best to do sober.) By the time I crept out of my parking space to head home, I was beginning to feel sick to my stomach. Having trouble focusing because I was seeing double, I closed one eye as I moved down the street. My clever trick didn't work; now I was seeing double out of just one eye. Willing myself to drive well, and just drunk enough to believe I could do it, I began to gain confidence. Unfortunately, like all those who drink too much, one of the first things to go is our good judgment.

Though I believed I was succeeding, I cringed when I heard the scraping of metal against metal as I sideswiped a hideous blue Ford Fairlane parked along the far left side of J Street, a three-lane, one-way thoroughfare.

Oh no, I thought, *I can't get caught.*

Though I'd tried to convince myself I wasn't that drunk, because I just wanted to get home, part of me knew full well that I shouldn't have been driving. I knew I'd wronged someone, and I was terrified of getting caught.

So I ran.

As I hurried off, my mind continued to race.

I know that man walking down the street saw what just happened, and can probably identify my car.

But I've been drinking, and if I get caught I'll be in big trouble.

I've got to keep moving.

Maybe they'll never find me.

Afraid to drive straight home, imagining police officers showing up at my mom's house at three in the morning, I drove to the home of a friend who let me park my car in his garage. Circling the car to survey the damage, I saw that my left headlight was turned askew, and there was a streak of turquoise paint on the side of my car.

Without a way to get home, I crashed at my friend's house that night. The moment I woke up in the morning, I was filled with remorse. Dragging myself to a sitting position, my mind flooded with the events from the previous night. *What the heck did I do?!* For the first time in a long time, I really felt the weight of my actions.

I screwed up.

I was drunk.

I wronged somebody.

I ran.

What if I'd hit a person instead of a car?!

In what I have to believe was conviction from the Holy Spirit, I had a very keen awareness that I was at a crossroads. And I considered the previous night's debacle to be a warning I was being invited to heed. Convicted, I knew I'd been lucky but that I couldn't continue down the path I was traveling. My life felt like a roller coaster of being in God's will for a moment, and then roaring off in my own way.

Reaching toward the bedside table, I grabbed a Bible I'd noticed as I was closing my eyes the night before. Normally I'm not the kind of person to believe I could close my eyes, flip open a Bible, and point to a magical verse as if it were a fortune cookie with a personalized message for me. But that morning, when I opened the well-worn King James Bible that seemed to have been left just for me, I turned to a Scripture that I believe was from the Lord.

Jeremiah 51:6 called out to my heart, "Flee out of the midst of Babylon, and deliver every man his soul: be not cut off in her iniquity; for this *is* the time of the LORD'S vengeance; he will render unto her a recompense."

My heart thumped in my chest as I heard God's voice speaking directly to me, inviting me to flee from my sinful ways. I heard God's voice as clearly as I ever had until that moment. Falling to the floor on my knees, I prayed to the One who had been so patient with me.

God, I can't keep doing this. And I know that I can't not do it without your help. I don't want to keep living like this, always running. Help me change. Help me be different.

I meant what I'd prayed, but my mind was still gripped by the deceiver. And by that I mean that I allowed myself to be deceived by the twisted reasoning that is the hallmark of the enemy.

Because it had been alcohol that had gotten me into such a mess, I quit drinking for a week or two.

When I wasn't drinking, I'd snort coke, rationalizing the use because I couldn't drink. Coke, I reasoned, hadn't gotten me into trouble. Alcohol had.

When I'd snorted so much coke that my nose was bleeding, I realized I was using too much. So I reasoned, "I'll just drink wine. Or champagne."

To me, this kind of thinking seemed entirely rational.

If you know an addict, the logic that sounds coconuts crazy to other people truly seems reasonable to us. While anyone on the outside could have easily seen the ways I was being controlled by various substances, I always believed I was in control of what I was using.

During that season, I had fooled myself into believing I really had my life together. But I was like one of those frogs who hops into a pot of room-temperature water and, as it begins to boil, doesn't have the good sense to hop out. Despite all the signs, I couldn't even see I was in the fire.

While I had what the apostle Paul calls "a form of godliness" (2 Timothy 3:5), I was, also in Paul's words, "denying its power." Not only did I allow myself to believe I was walking with God, but the dream in my heart was to make it big as a country gospel singer. And if you know country gospel—or any kind of gospel!—that means I sang about God's power to transform lives. I saw no incongruity between my lifestyle and the words I sang about God and truly believed. If there was an internal tug of war in my heart between the lifestyle to which I was addicted and releasing it all to God, during that season my lifestyle was definitely winning.

Has there been a season in your life when you felt tugged in two directions? Maybe the Spirit was after you, and might even have been speaking quite clearly, but you weren't ready to listen. Like me, you might have believed that you could muscle your way into achieving the dream you so desperately wanted. You believed you could achieve your goals in your own strength. But God isn't about endorsing a life that doesn't honor Him. Though I didn't know it at the time, God wanted so much more for me than I wanted for myself. God wanted me not just to succeed, but to thrive. To be well. To be whole.

Part of me knew it was time for me to look inside my own heart and allow God to heal the hurting places. But moment by moment, it was easier to numb the pain than to do the hard work of being vulnerable before God and allowing him to heal me. So I continued to drink and use because I wasn't yet ready to receive the fullness of God's gracious mercy for a sinner like me.

As I toiled away at Fridays, scoring the occasional weekend singing gig, my dream of making it big in Nashville was never far from my mind. So, once again, I packed my car to the ceiling, donned my light camel-colored Resistol cowboy hat, and set off from Sacramento. Driving through Colorado, I headed down to Nashville with an ice chest filled with wine on the floor of the passenger's seat. Because I'd worked at TGI Fridays in Sacramento, I knew a job would be waiting for me in Nashville. My black pants and signature red-and-white striped uniform even got me a few nights of work at restaurants along the route.

Two weeks after I left home, I arrived in Nashville, with a single thought pulsing through my head: *I'm gonna make it big.*

I was twenty-two the first time I moved to Nashville, and I was the consummate stereotype of the starry-eyed girl trying to make it in Music City. Wearing my favorite cowboy boots, jeans, and a denim jacket, I hustled up and down Music Row, knocking on doors and hoping for my big break. My black leather portfolio was loaded with promo packages that included my demo bio, demo tape, and my 8x10 headshot. The first stop at any recording label was always talking to the receptionist at the desk.

"Good morning," I'd chirp with a smile. "Who is your A&R?" (I was asking who in their company was their "artist and representation" agent.)

On a good day, I'd make it past the desk and get to speak to someone in person. I'd introduce myself, mention a few of my talent show wins, and leave my promo package.

On a bad day, the gal at the desk wouldn't let me through. She'd politely take my package, but I suspected that after I left she'd put it in a deep well with the other three thousand promo packages wannabe stars had naively left with her. Most likely a wannabe herself, she had no reason to make sure I was seen.

Ostensibly, my Nashville life was about making enough money at Fridays to allow me to pursue my dream of becoming an inspirational country music singer. That's what I had set out to do when I left Sacramento. That's what I let my mom believe was still my goal, when we spoke on the phone.

In large part, it was true. Anytime I had a day off I'd go downtown to network with people in the industry and share my demos. If I wasn't singing in a showcase, I'd go to friends' showcases to lend them support. And they'd do the same for me.

"Hey, I'm singing at the Bluebird Café tonight, come hear me."

"I'll be at Third and Lindsley, come hear me."

"Come out to Tootsies tonight at nine to hear me."

One night I had the opportunity to sing "You're The Reason God Made Oklahoma" with David Frizelle at the Nashville Palace. Afterward, I stepped out behind the Palace to chat with him. Because I knew I'd really nailed it, I fell asleep that night wondering if he'd take me on the road with him. I knew it would only take one little break like that to get noticed. He didn't invite me to tour with him, but certainly every gig I played, I hoped the right person would hear me. Would love me. Would include me. Would represent me. So no matter where I was, whether I'd traveled there by car or by foot, I had my promo packages with me.

Whenever I'd meet an agent or have a promising conversation with a producer, I'd call my mom to dish about it. While I was genuinely excited every time, it was almost as if I needed her to know that I was doing what I'd set out to do.

But there was a huge part of my life I never shared with her, though I always suspected she might know.

My friend Rosie and I had started doing lines of cocaine back in California. And when I visited my dad in Concord, I realized he had a source for cocaine, so we did it together.

When I moved to Nashville, my father became my supplier. I'd send him a check in the mail and he would send me an ounce of cocaine in pure rock form via Federal Express. I'd pay him anywhere from six hundred to eight hundred dollars for that rock. We'd both track the package, and when it was delivered, I'd would pick it up at the FedEx office. Because sending illegal drugs through the mail was a federal offense, part of me always expected that dogs would sniff out the drugs and I'd be handcuffed the moment I entered the building.

It never happened.

Once I got home, relieved to be a free woman for another day, I had to cut the rock and chop it. Or I'd put it through a strainer, using a marble pulce to grind it into a powder. If the coke wasn't ground finely enough, the grainy crystals would be inhaled and burn one's mucus membranes. But a finely ground powder would travel all the way through one's system, providing the sought-after rush.

While I was definitely cutting the coke to enjoy myself, I was also selling it. At $100 per gram, I'd typically triple my investment. So once I'd processed it, I'd set aside enough to get me through until the next package from Concord would arrive. Though I'd cut the powder I sold with baking powder, I kept the pure stuff for myself.

The consummate entrepreneur, I'd carefully weigh the coke on a triple-beam scale and fold up a gram into a rectangle of white wax paper into a secure origami shape. I'd keep these in my purse, which I always tucked on a shelf behind the bar so I could keep an eye on it. I was proud of the reputation I'd developed as many people's go-to when they needed the real stuff.

Some of my customers were fellow Fridays employees. Others were customers. Some were fat cats who had worked for Elvis. Owners of other bars bought from me. And chronic partiers. And this was before a client could simply text a purposely vague request for drugs.

So a buyer at the bar would ask, "You got one?"

I'd nod, to let them know I did.

Or a bartender would ask, "Hey, you got anything for me?"

Carefully placing a small waxy package between the folds of a beverage napkin, I'd slide the napkin across the bar to him, placing their drink of choice on top of it.

Typically, when someone steps up to the bar for a drink, we'd spin the beverage napkin and it would land right in front of them. So when one of my customers who wanted to buy showed up with four friends, I spun four of the napkins in front of them, and carefully slid one in his direction. I'd pat it with my hand as I took their orders. So although my mouth was saying "What can I get you to drink?" my eyes and my body were saying, "It's in here. Don't lift this up."

I was making good money, and had even saved ten grand, so the whole thing was working for me. I liked having money in the bank and coke in my pocket. It made me feel powerful.

Drinking also continued to make me feel pretty good. After just about every evening shift at Fridays, it was *party time*. The kitchen closed at 1 a.m., and the bar closed at two o'clock. That's when the fun began. On my twenty-third birthday, I'd worked a day shift. That didn't stop me from loading up on a few "Daggwoods" before going out to meet friends. Rather than using a straw, the proper way to drink a Daggwood was to sip near the lemon wedges, because it made the Absolut Vodka go down without a burn.

After a couple of those, I stepped out into the rain and ducked into my car to go to Benihanas. With no thought of the evening just a year or so earlier when I'd sideswiped a parked car and vowed to God that I wanted to live differently, I once again drove drunk. Beautiful Belle Meade Boulevard, a street lined with gorgeous mansions on both sides and a greenway in the center, was in the "old money" part of town. Two lanes of traffic ran in each direction. I didn't see a stop sign on the boulevard and started breezing through the intersection. Suddenly realizing I wasn't alone there, I slammed on the brakes and hydroplaned about fifty yards before careening into a ditch and wrapping my VW Rabbit around a tree.

When the paramedics arrived, I was still in shock. Both my knees had hit the dash, and my stockings were torn and bloody. Blood was also pouring from my mouth because I'd bit my tongue on impact, nearly severing it. I was still in a daze as medical workers loaded me onto a stretcher and transported me to the hospital.

Though my tongue was already swelling, I remember being examined in the emergency room, and telling the doctor I didn't have insurance. In reality, I did have insurance at Fridays; I was just freaked out by the whole thing. I waited for the doctor to leave the room and then got up and left. I found a phone in a hallway and called one of my friends to come get me. When we arrived at my home, a whole crowd of friends were waiting to go to Benihanas to celebrate my birthday. In one of many absurd moments of the evening, my awkward swollen-tongue explanation about what had just happened was interrupted by a phone call from my mom, who was excited to wish me a happy birthday. Speaking like I had about forty pieces of bubble gum in my mouth, I explained to her that I'd had an accident and couldn't talk because of my big "thung." Somehow, she understood me. Like moms do.

Still dazed and confused, I sent everyone out without me. That night and the next day I went through a box and a half of Kleenex, wiping up the blood that kept coming out of my mouth.

The bleeding mouth really was a great snapshot of my life at that moment. What I'd been putting into my mouth—booze and pills— kept getting me into trouble, and now *injury*. And somehow I was completely powerless, unable to stop the hemorrhaging. This wasn't something that someone else was doing to me. I wasn't a helpless victim who was unable to defend herself. I wasn't a child. I was making choices that were harming me and others. Some part of me could see that, but I didn't know how to stop.

When we don't deal with the buried pain in our lives, it doesn't go away. While it would be nice if time healed all wounds, what happens more often is that old wounds are left to fester in darkness.

They pulse and throb. They cause us to limp and stumble. I chose to self-medicate, numbing myself to the evident infection inside me. What I needed most was healing. What I chose instead was anesthesia.

Perhaps there are red flags in your own life that are begging for your attention. It may be that you're beginning to finally hear the concerns of a parent, a spouse, a child. Or you've become increasingly aware of a sadness within you. Maybe your eyes have even been opened to the ways your old hurts are impacting your present relationships. These can all be signals that a buried hurt stands in need of healing. Although uncomfortable, this is actually a tender mercy. As we notice the aches and pains in our hearts, God is waiting for us to place them in His healing hands. For some, that will mean seeking the help of a professional counselor. And for others it might be a simple one-word prayer, "Help!"

I, though, was not yet ready for heart healing.

Chapter 9

SO CLOSE

It's no secret that in a city like Los Angeles, there's a pretty good possibility that your barista at Starbucks or your waiter at Jerry's Deli is a budding actor or actress who rush between auditions on their days off, in the hopes of landing their big break in Hollywood. In fact, it's so common that there's actually a term for it: WAM, meaning "Waitress, Actress, Model." The Nashville equivalent of that, in my experience, was wanna-be stars working in restaurants, bars, and offices, hustling for gigs and opportunities in our off-hours.

So when one of my girlfriends who shared my big dreams suggested putting together an all-girl band, I was in. My landlord, Bob, was our manager. His secretary—also his mistress—was in the band. A girl named Pam, who worked as a secretary for the band Alabama, joined us. And a fourth, Sylvia, worked alongside me at Friday's as a hostess.

We called ourselves Heartland and we sang Top 40 country hits in four-part harmony. Live audiences loved us, but the dream, of course, was a record deal.

Touring money.

Recording money.

Promotions.

Marketing.

Had our dreams come true, we would have been invited to record with MCA, Sony, Capitol, Curb, or Warner Brothers. Or we might have been discovered by Reba McEntire's entertainment company, Starstruck. I also would have loved to have been picked up by one of the Christian labels, like Reunion or Word.

The only other four-girl group I knew of were the Forester sisters. Our vibe and our four-part harmony was similar to theirs, but cuter. Heartland's style was shiny country glitz: rhinestone chokers, one big heart earring, hair as high as we could get it, and black leather skirts. We cut some songs in the studio, and we were actually pretty good!

It was the mid-eighties, and we watched other artists living the dream for which we were reaching. We kept our eyes on women like Reba, Wynonna, Naomi—ones who didn't even need last names. We followed the top country acts like Anne Murray, Shania Twain, Juice Newton, Crystal Gale, Vince Gill, and Randy Travis.

But nothing big happened for us.

Just as there is never a clear, foolproof path to success, there are countless reasons why an artist or group doesn't make it. It was hard coordinating the schedules of three single gals and one married one. Our manager wasn't as well-networked as those dedicated solely to the industry. Although we didn't dwell on it at the time, girl groups weren't as hot as guy groups. I'm sure my drinking and using didn't help. Not during rehearsals. Not before our photo shoot. Not after gigs. After about a year, we discovered what hundreds of other starry-eyed hopefuls also figured out: talent wasn't enough.

As Heartland disbanded, I was more discouraged than ever because my dreams weren't coming true. I'd tried to catch a break as a solo artist. I'd done the girl band. I was singing demos for other people so writers could pitch them to execs for another artist to land. I even sang songs for Lorrie Morgan's brother, Marty Morgan. And although I wasn't yet ready to own it, part of me realized I was an alcoholic. And an addict.

I was done. I'd had a string of broken relationships in Nashville that had left me brokenhearted. I'd given it my best shot and I was releasing my dreams of stardom.

When I packed up all of my things to return to California, it wasn't going to be a "respite" trip to gather up my confidence and return to Nashville. I was really done.

When I vowed to swear off the music business, I was also trying to release my self-destructive lifestyle. In my mind, the two went hand in hand. I believed the "business" was fueling the instability in my life and making it unmanageable. That logic, relieving me of some of the responsibility for my own choices, really worked for me.

In my mind, I was leaving my old life behind, and would be starting fresh back in California. What I didn't yet realize is that the same way your clothes get packed up in a suitcase to travel with you to your new destination, your vices get packed as well. So I was as surprised as anyone when, just three months after moving back, I was right back in the middle of the life I thought I'd left behind. While I recognized the destructive pull in my life, and the ways clubs and the music scene could feed that, I also knew God had knit music deeply into the fibers of who I am, and that there was something *good* about that.

One weekend I'd gone up to The Nugget in South Lake Tahoe to hear this all-girl band play. When we were talking after their set, they said they were looking for one more girl. Crystal, one of the group members, had heard me sing, and I was hired on the spot. I started doing shows with them the following week.

Nothing about my drinking and using had changed.

Not long after I joined the group, I was partying in Sacramento. Actually, "partying" is just a glamorous way of saying that I continued to drink after my shift as a master bartender at Friday's, where I was making pretty good money. I'd been barhopping in the Citrus Heights Sunrise area, where I'd hit a few places by the mall. I was good friends with the bartender at Bobby McGees, and I was heading to see him at about 1:20 a.m., when I decided it was actually time for me to head home.

No sooner had I made an illegal U-turn to head home than I recognized the flashing red-and-blue lights in my rearview mirror. Pulling onto a side street in the residential neighborhood, I turned off my engine and prepared to charm whatever officer was about to approach my car. As the officer was taking down my license plate number I reached into the glove compartment for my car registration and rifled through my purse to dig my license out of my wallet.

This wasn't my first rodeo. In fact, I'd gotten plenty of experience talking my way out of tickets when I'd been pulled over in Nashville.

Say your ABCs. Typically, I'd sing them.

Walk in a straight line. Can do.

How much have you had to drink? A few glasses of wine.

"A few glasses of wine" is *always* the right answer.

Drive safely.

With many opportunities to perform, I'd become quite adept at demonstrating how *not* loaded I was.

After I'd jumped through all the hoops, the officer would ask me where I was going. And no matter where I had actually been heading—usually to another bar—I would assure them sweetly that I was going home. "Home" is *always* the right answer.

I was pinching my license and registration between my fingers when a tall officer with dark hair approached my vehicle.

"Good evening, officer," I said in a sweet drawl.

All business, he ordered, "License and registration, please."

Handing him the documents, I noted his terse manner.

After verifying the documents, he shined his flashlight in my face. While I was playing the part of the sweet sober driver, my eyes—watery, a bit red, way too relaxed—gave me away. Had I been sober, I probably could have recognized that my altered speech was probably giving me away as well.

"Please step out of the car, ma'am," the officer ordered.

"Of course," I willingly obliged. I knew that this was where I really shined.

But the laws were stricter in California than in Tennessee, and all the charm in the world wasn't going to get me out of this one. After putting me through a brief battery of tests, the officer finally returned to his car and came back with a breathalyzer.

One look at the officer's face while he read the results told me that this was definitely not a "drive home safely" situation. In fact, I was so intoxicated that I was handcuffed and taken directly downtown.

Once I was charged with driving under the influence of alcohol, I was put into dry hold for twelve hours before they let me call a friend to come pick me up. I started with Randy, the bartender at Bobby McGees, but he couldn't come, so he sent his brother to pick me up and help me find my car. Because I couldn't remember the name of the street where I'd parked it, the hunt took us several hours.

In a world where I learned from my mistakes, this arrest would have been the *real* wakeup I needed to get my drinking under control. But that was not a world I was living in. Instead, I convinced myself I just needed to eat food before I drank. *That* was the big problem, I reasoned: not enough eating. Or I'd tell myself I needed to limit my drinking to wine—to those proverbial "few glasses" that never really seemed to be just a few.

I really believed what I was telling myself.

In fact, seventeen days after my arrest, I had myself so convinced that I could manage my drinking that when my friend Nikki returned from a Special Ops assignment in Korea, I had a bottle of champagne chilling on ice in the front seat when I went to pick her up from the airport! I was wearing a little black Nicole Miller dress and a soft, feathery, white African marabou wrap with heels. Nikki, blonde hair cascading past her shoulders, had changed into a red dress for our girls' night out.

The champagne wasn't the end of it. I also had a baggy full of rock cocaine in my purse and a gun I'd bought in Nashville, a .38 that was shoved between my seat and the center console.

Nikki and I had already been doing coke when I zipped over the summit, speeding into the town of Meyers. Though I'd passed no less than three signs announcing that the speed limit was thirty-five miles per hour, I was so caught up in fun conversation and partying I didn't even see them. That's when I saw the familiar red-and-blue lights.

I pulled over quickly, preparing for my big show.

When the officer moseyed over to the passenger side of the car, Nikki put her window down and stepped out of the passenger door. In my head I was thinking, *Don't get outta the car, Nikki!*

Glancing into the car at me, the cop asked, "You know why I'm stopping you?"

I caught his eyes as he glanced down at the champagne tub on the passenger floorboard. Still corked, I hoped for the best.

"No, officer," I answered innocently.

"I stopped you because you were speeding," he explained.

"I'm sorry," I said. "I guess I didn't realize. My friend just returned from doing a tour of duty overseas and I guess we're just anxious to get to the casinos to celebrate."

As the officer looked around the car, he noticed that the mirror, dirty with cocaine residue, had slid out from under the passenger seat into view.

"Girls, girls," he chimed, like a disappointed father, "how much of this white stuff on the mirror have you had?"

That was the moment when I realized I wasn't quite as smart as I thought I was.

Stepping away from the car, he spoke into his radio, and within what felt like moments, we were surrounded by marked and unmarked cars from the Drug Enforcement Agency. Meyers is the little town before the split in the road that leads either to the casino or around the lake. There's a guard stop there, directing traffic, and it is crawling with California Highway Patrol officers. Suddenly, it seemed like every officer in the state had swarmed my car like flies on poop.

The officer asked us to get out of the car and to sit beside the road. That was my vantage point as I watched countless agents and dogs search my car. To say they were thorough is an understatement. They opened Nikki's duffle bags. They rifled through every one of my bags in the trunk. They found the cocaine in my purse. To their credit, I suppose, they searched every single inch of my vehicle. I mean, they found inches I didn't even know existed.

Knowing that Nikki was still clocked in on military duty until she reached home, I scrambled to think how she could avoid the ugly consequences I knew were coming. I couldn't let her take any of the blame.

"This is all mine," I pled with the officers. "I just picked her up and she didn't know about any of this."

Once again I felt and heard the ominous click of handcuffs being secured behind my back, as one of the officers spoke in a monotone voice, "You have the right to remain silent . . ."

Nikki was allowed to drive my car away from the scene and get a hotel for the night.

I, on the other hand, spent another night in lockup. I won't lie: I was the best-dressed girl in jail that night. After a night in dry hold, with a new DUI *and* a charge for possession of illegal drugs, I made seven or eight calls until I found somebody who could bail me out.

Doug, the same guy who'd done it seventeen days earlier, was the lucky winner.

Because I'd left my fancy Vuarnet sunglasses in the back of the cop car, I asked the station to contact the arresting officer for me. He brought them by the station before Nikki and I headed back down the mountain to Sacramento.

Recognizing me in the parking lot, the cop came over to my car.

"I'm so sorry all this happened," he said.

Which seems like it broke some kind of police-officer oath.

He continued, "You seem like a nice girl."

It seemed like that one was up for grabs.

Startled, still feeling so ashamed, I could only mumble a weak, "Thanks."

"I'm sorry all this crap happened to you."

"Me, too," I answered, with a little chuckle.

"But I just gotta ask you something . . ." he continued.

"Sure," I said. "What is it?"

"Where did you hide the gun?"

I was dumbfounded.

"Gun?" I hedged. "What do you mean?"

That was the one thing I thought I'd gotten away with! There was no way I was going to admit to him or anyone else that I'd had a gun in the car.

He continued, "I had my guys search your car, and they didn't find it."

When I'd watched them search the car the previous night, I had breathed a prayer that they wouldn't find it, and I knew that if they had, I would have heard about it. The big question, in my mind, was how on earth he knew about it? And if he knew, why hadn't I been charged?

"I didn't see it," he explained, "until I looked back inside for the pen I dropped in your car, after they'd searched."

"Uhh ..." I hedged, trying to buy time to come up with an excuse.

He read the look of astonishment on my face, and explained, "I thought, 'She's been through enough.' "

What?! Overlooking an illegal firearm possession seemed a hundred times worse for a police officer to do than apologizing for my rough night.

"So I just walked away," he concluded.

I didn't know what to say.

"Well," I replied, "thank you."

He gave a silent nod before driving away.

The gun part of my big mess felt like a small gift I didn't deserve. When I received paperwork detailing my arrests in the mail, I realized I'd also received a second gift: because the court system was moving so slowly in California, both arrests were booked as "first offenses." So while the most recent arrest should technically have been my second, it was still filed as a "first offense."

As my bad breaks continued to rack up, one of the biggest breaks of my career was about to unfold.

When I'd been singing with Crystal's band, a scout named Larry Walker had been sent to check us out by the woman who schedules tours for the Department of Defense. I'd overheard a bit of this gentleman's conversation with Crystal after the gig.

"Is this a duo?" he'd asked her, having heard each of us sing that evening. I'd sung "The Sweetest Thing I've Ever Known is Loving You," by Juice Newton.

I can see why he thought we might be a duo. We'd set the piano up like a string machine, so I'd play the chords, that would sound like strings, starting the tempo and running the programs. At night she'd pound out the bass notes on another keyboard, that we'd record onto a machine since we didn't have a bass player.

When the scout asked her if we were a duo, she answered, "No, it's my band."

Nodding toward me, he quickly shot back, "Then don't let her come out in front and sing."

But Larry really connected with me, and even began helping me with bookings. He actually had a clever little routine to get people into my shows. He'd come into town with flyers for the gigs, and ask people on the street, "What are you doing tonight? You gonna be at Winners? Did you know *Lisa Daggs* is gonna be there?!" He said my name with the same inflection one might use to announce the Queen of England.

"You haven't heard of her?!" he'd add. "You're kidding me! She's the best female vocalist in Northern California."

He was the perfect hype man!

One day Larry called me about putting together a new band.

"Lisa," he raved, "you've really got the goods."

They were the kind of words I'd longed to hear from agents and labels for years.

So Larry, who had connections in Vegas, helped put together a new band called Lisa Daggs and a Touch of Class. (Because everything about wild hair, short skirts, and tux tails said *class*!)

Not only was Lisa Daggs and a Touch of Class getting gigs locally, but Larry had lined up the Department of Defense tour for us! Over the holidays we were scheduled to sing to military personnel in Japan, Australia, and several other stops around the globe.

I was over the moon about going on tour. Everyone in the band and crew was busy getting passports, rehearsing, and prepping all the gear to be shipped.

It was finally happening.

I was about to go on tour.

I was ready to live the dream.

I could taste it.

One weekend that we had a gig in Tahoe, the U-Haul was all packed up with our gear in the driveway and I was sitting in my mom's kitchen waiting for another girl in the band to come over so we could leave. Flipping mindlessly through the paper, I could hear my mom coming down the wooden hallway. I assumed she wanted to say goodbye and wish me luck.

When I saw her face as she stepped into the kitchen, it did not look like the face of a woman wanting to give me a hug and wish me the best. I saw pain. I saw disappointment. And even a momentary flash of anger. It was a look I was coming to know well.

A week earlier I'd been searching the house for my amethyst ring, and my mom had been helping me. Because I knew it had been on my finger that day, we were both going from room to room peeking under furniture, reaching into sofa cracks, and scanning carpets for the tiniest glimmer of purple. She was on her hands and knees beside my bed when she discovered my pipe and other paraphernalia. So I recognized the look.

I was bent over putting my tennis shoes on when my mom appeared in the opening of the pocket doorway between the kitchen and the dining room. My heart fell when I glanced up and saw her holding my signature brown and gold Louis Vuitton zipper change purse, where I'd been keeping my drugs. The change purse had been on a pile of personal items I'd hauled to the kitchen that was waiting to be packed into the truck. When she tossed it in my direction, I watched it spiral toward me in slow motion before landing in my lap with the weight of the world and my mother's broken heart.

With a twinge of despair, she simply said, "You dropped your drugs."

I was without words.

Grabbing the offending pouch, I shoved it in my back pocket, if only to get it out of sight.

My friend was at the door, and so my mom grabbed a final laundry basket of items from the kitchen floor and walked us out to the rental truck.

After my friend walked around to the passenger side of the vehicle, my mom looked me in the eye and said just five words, "I fear for your future."

Her voice sank into my heart like a dagger. But there was nothing aggressive or unkind about what she'd said. I heard only concern. Waving goodbye, reaching for the knob on the car radio, I turned on the music to mute the words that hand landed forcefully in my heart.

When we returned from our Tahoe gig, and were making final preparations to perform overseas, I went to a little bar in the Rosemont area, called The Mushroom, to have a few cocktails. And of course by "a few," I mean "more than a few." High on cocaine, I hadn't slept in ten days and I was exhausted. Honestly, I felt like I deserved something to take the edge off. But when I left the joint,

I didn't notice I'd left my teal leather clutch behind. The next morning, when I couldn't find it, I realized what had happened. Because my purse contained my "valuables," I hoped the person who found it had just handed it over to the staff.

When I thought the bar would be open the next day, I drove back and spoke to the owner.

"Hey, I was here last night and left a teal clutch," I explained to him. "Any chance someone turned it in?" I asked.

With an expression that told me he was unmoved by my story, he simply announced, "You'll have to get it from the sheriff's department."

That's right. Ironically, while a police officer had been willing to overlook an illegal firearm, the bar owner wasn't going to let me off the hook. Rather than looking the other way, and simply handing over my purse, he made sure I'd be held responsible. I later learned he was in recovery. (That's right, he was a tee-totaling bar owner!)

When I heard the words "sheriff's department," a crude word may have passed my lips.

I mentally reviewed the contents I remembered being in my purse:

- Lipstick
- Powder
- My driver's license
- A Ziploc baggie that contained several grams of coke.

The coke was folded up, origami-style, to be sold in case someone was looking to score that night.

Having no idea what to do next, I got back in my Celica and drove and drove around my mom's neighborhood, desperately trying to think of a plan to get me out of the most recent mess I'd made.

What am I going to do?!

Although I wasn't yet ready to admit it, I was living the life of an addict. My world was chaotic, lacking any semblance of discipline. I did what felt good.

It was Sunday, November 11, 1989.

On the inside, I felt like a little girl who'd gotten in trouble at school, and I wanted nothing more than to go home and curl up in my mother's lap. But when I approached her house, I saw a police car out front and an officer speaking to my mom at the front door.

What do I do?!

Because of my prior arrests, I wasn't even supposed to be driving. I circled around the block and then pulled in front of a neighbor's house, to keep watching. When the officer turned to return to his car, I saw the teal purse in his hand.

What have I done?!

Glancing in the rearview mirror, I was surprised by what I saw. My hair was brittle and dry. My skin was gray. I was exhausted and a part of me knew I wasn't going to be able to talk my way out of this one. While I'd always prided myself on being the master of getting out of trouble, I sensed it was over. I watched the officer walk down the cement path toward his car, and I pulled into my mom's driveway.

Getting out of my car, I addressed him saying, through tears, "I think you're looking for me."

"Are you Lisa?" he asked.

"Yeah," I admitted.

"And is this your purse?" he asked, holding out my clutch.

"Yeah," answered.

"And are these your drugs?" he queried, opening the purse to show me what I already knew was inside.

I could have lied. The purse had been out of my possession and I knew I could have denied they were mine. But I was finally done.

"Yeah," I confessed, eyes to the ground.

Pulling out my license, he looked at the picture, and then looked at me. He looked back at the picture, and then looked again at me.

Finally, he weighed in, "You look like hell."

He wasn't wrong.

"Yeah," I admitted, "I'm pretty tired."

We continued to talk in front of my mom's house for the next forty-five minutes, me sharing my heart with him.

I'm tired.

I want to quit.

I can't.

I sing for a living.

I'm tired of all this.

And for a minute, I thought he was going to let me go.

But in the end, he said, "Well, I'm going to have to take you downtown."

He handcuffed me in front of my mom's house before assisting me into the back of his car.

"I have to say," he told me, "I think you're probably the most honest person I've ever arrested."

So I had that going for me.

When I was processed at the police station, I was taken into a private room to be strip-searched. Bending over so my "cavities" could be checked was absolutely humiliating. If I thought I'd hit bottom before, this was rock bottom. I was put into a holding cell, but was then allowed to make one phone call.

"Hey, Mom," I said, feeling so ashamed, "it's Lisa, and I'm at the police station."

Like any mom worth her salt, she weighed in immediately.

"I told you you weren't supposed to be driving . . ." she began.

"Actually, mom," I explained, "it's worse than that."

When I'd been running from the Lord's plan for my life, I'd fooled myself into believing I didn't have a problem. That I was in control of my drinking and using. That I wasn't addicted like other users. But the signs were all there.

I'd been arrested for a DUI. Twice.

I'd been charged for drug possession. Twice.

I went days without sleeping.

There weren't days when I wasn't drinking or using.

And now my mom's fears for my life were unfolding before our eyes.

All the signs were there, but I squeezed my eyes shut and refused to see them.

Though I didn't know it at the time, when we are living far from the Lord, there are always clues that we've strayed from Him.

Maybe a relative's innocent web browser search exposed our dirty little habit.

Maybe we get a bad review at work because our late nights have led to late mornings.

Maybe we discover we have an STD.

Maybe our relationships have suffered because we've prioritized destructive behavior over the people in our lives who matter most.

Maybe our bank account is drained because we've had to use our savings to dig ourselves out of the hole we've chosen for ourselves.

When we've abandoned the Lord's path for our lives, when we've forsaken the goodness of His ways, there will always be clues. Signals. Signs.

The twenty-seventh Proverb says, "The prudent see danger and take refuge, but the simple keep going and pay the penalty" (Proverbs 27:12). I admit, I was the simple one who refused to "see" the danger I was in and take refuge. Each arrest, each discovery at home, had been an opportunity for me to find refuge. To seek the Lord. To be transformed. But, hardheaded, I refused each one.

Are there signs today that your life has become unmanageable? Have the people who love you noticed that you're teetering on the edge? Have they expressed their concern for you? While conviction is always uncomfortable, I believe the Spirit uses people, circumstances, and consequences to open our eyes to see what is most real, and most true.

That's what God does.

God opens our eyes—through people, through prayer, through Scripture—to finally "see" the reality of the choices we've made.

I'd been given chance after chance to pause, consider the direction my life was going, and reconfigure my course. But again and again, my arrogance convinced me I could sweet-talk my way out of any trouble in which I found myself.

But this time was different.

Chapter 10

CONSEQUENCES OF COMPROMISE

" I don't belong in here."

The words pounded in my head as I nervously glanced at the women whose company I shared while I was locked up overnight in the county jail. Although I'd been locked up before, these women were really *rough*. Cranksters, strung out on meth, rocked back and forth. Others were picking at sores and scabs on their faces, and arms. I viewed these women as society's refuse, and I was nothing like them. I had talent. I had promise. I was preparing to represent my country on tour serving the U.S. military. I didn't belong among addicts who'd thrown their lives and relationships away to score the next hit.

Addicts have a genius way of convincing ourselves that we don't have a problem. And the fact that my physical health, my spiritual life, my relationships, and my career were all on the verge of collapse wasn't enough to open my eyes. I was so far gone that I was even able to justify the days when I would use a thousand dollars of rock cocaine and still truly believe I was different from the meth-heads who shared my cell.

But unable to medicate reality away, unable to walk out of the jail and smoke a rock, I was forced to face what my life was in that moment. I'd been arrested four times, and my life was out of control. As each hour ticked by, my stubborn "I don't belong here" morphed into a prayer of desperation.

How did I get here?

God, where did I go wrong?

What have I done?

Why is this happening to me?

Professionally, I was on the precipice of success. I had booked an international tour. The thing I'd worked so hard for was finally within reach.

As my eyelids grew heavy and my racing mind began to settle, I heard the Lord's voice answering the questions that swirled in my heart. After being locked up for about twelve hours, a single word from the Lord: *compromise.*

How did you get here? Compromise.

Where did you go wrong? Compromise.

What have you done? Compromise.

Why is this happening to you? Compromise. Because of your compromise, these are your consequences.

As the words penetrated, I was forced to face the truth. No one had done this to me. No one had dragged me against my will. No one except me made the choice, night after night, to booze and use. I had made those choices. I had compromised what I knew was right in order to feel good for another minute. Another hour. Another day. Days had rolled into weeks, and weeks had rolled into months.

I'd compromised my morals.

I'd compromised my heart.

I'd compromised my health.

I'd compromised my integrity.

I'd compromised my faith.

I'd compromised my relationships, especially with my mom.

When I was high, or chasing the high, I'd done things I'd sworn I'd never do.

And although I'd been willing to compromise everything I believed in, the truth never left me.

In my darkest hours, I knew that Jesus was the Son of God.

I understood He had died on the cross for my sins.

I trusted there was none above Him.

I believed all of that in my head, and even in my heart. But because of my behavior, because of my rebellious choices, I wasn't allowing God access to my will. Although I knew beyond a shadow of a doubt that Jesus was the Savior of the world, I would not allow Him to save *me*.

And although my compromise had compromised God's access to me, I would discover for myself what I'd heard in church: that we are never beyond God's reach.

As I began to accept the reality of what I'd done, I began to parrot the words I'd spoken to God so many other times.

If You get me out of this mess, I promise I'll quit using and I'll never quit telling people what You've done for me. Lord, I just need one more chance.

Although I didn't know exactly what kind of sentence I might be facing, I had reason to believe that I'd be going to prison for three to five years. In those terrifying moments, I was as scared as I'd ever been.

The next day I had to call my mom to bail me out. Humbled, I told her to look in a box beneath my dresser where I'd stashed about five hundred dollars, in case we needed it to get me released. When she arrived, though, they released me into her custody on my own recognizance.

It was a very quiet ride home.

Back under my mother's roof, I continued strategizing how I'd pick up the broken pieces this time. I'd hired attorneys before to get me out of the messes I'd faced, but I never felt like I was getting my money's worth. So this time, while I'd been locked up, I'd requested a public defender who told me up front to start going to Narcotics Anonymous meetings and getting signatures from leaders there to prove I'd attended.

Although I was heartbroken at what I was putting my mom through, her steadfast commitment to me never wavered. The day after my release she accompanied me to my first Narcotics Anonymous meeting at Sutter Hospital in downtown Sacramento. One of the outspoken advocates for the program was the well-known Dr. Jerome Lackner, former California health director and leader in the addiction recovery community.

I marvel that I have any memory of the day at all, since it was my eleventh consecutive day with no sleep. Unlike some stricter meetings, this one, called an "open meeting," allowed guests like my mom to visit. It felt humiliating to have to ask the volunteer at the welcome desk where the meeting was being held. Everything in me wanted to tell her, "I don't belong here! I'm a good person." Resisting the urge, I simply received her directions: down the hall, make a right at the end, last door on the left. Slipping into the conference room, wanting to be invisible, I led us to two chairs near the back. While I expected the crowd to be a lot like the cranksters I'd seen in jail, it was actually more like a friendly fellowship hour after church. People smiled and chatted as they filled up their coffee cups, not as if they'd been sentenced to attend, but as if they wanted to be in that church, in that room, at that time. While I was still wrestling with attending, still unsure whether I belonged but hoping it would make a good impression on the court, everyone else I saw seemed to be there because they wanted to be.

When a leader stepped up front and called the gathering to order, someone read a few statements to start things off. With each word, I continued to ask the silent question, *Do I belong here?*

A middle-aged man in a dressy gray suit who looked like he could be the CEO of some Fortune 500 company read from a weathered green and gold book:

"Before coming to the Fellowship of NA, we could not manage our own lives. We could not live and enjoy life as other people do. We had to have something different and we thought we had found it in drugs. We placed their use ahead of the welfare of our families, our wives, husbands, and our children. We had to have drugs at all costs. We did many people great harm, but most of all we harmed ourselves. Through our inability to accept personal responsibilities we were actually creating our own problems. We seemed to be incapable of facing life on its own terms."

Despite my resistance, and no doubt aided by all the people who seemed normal, I was able to locate myself as someone who possibly "belonged." Maybe.

As the CEO read, scenes from my life flashed through my mind. Talking my way out of a DUI in Nashville. Sitting on the ground in my sexy black dress as Drug Enforcement agents searched my car outside Tahoe. I pictured the look on my mom's face when I'd stumble into the house loaded after a night of partying. Desperately gathering my money before meeting a dealer. Glancing around the room, seeing women and men who looked like teachers and coaches and parents and neighbors, I slowly began to soften. One young woman shared that she stole money from her mom to buy drugs. A man who looked to be in his fifties said that most of his romantic relationships over two decade, were impacted by drug use. Maybe I did belong, after all.

I was wildly impressed when I heard attendees announce, "I have thirty days clean," or "I have ninety days clean." I had no idea how they did it! I was in awe of their seemingly impossible achievement. And even though I couldn't imagine going even a week without using, their testimonies emboldened me and encouraged me to believe that another life was possible. I trusted them because their journeys gave them credibility.

After the meeting, several people stopped to greet me and my mom. Honestly, this crew was a lot friendlier than folks in a lot of churches I'd visited over the years! Before heading back out to the car, I sheepishly asked the man who'd called the meeting to order if he'd sign my sheet to confirm that I'd been there.

"Happy to," he said, taking the pen I extended to him. After scribbling his name, he added, "I hope we see you again, Lisa. You can do this."

While just the words of one sinner to another, they landed in my heart as if they'd been specially anointed just for me.

For the weeks between my release and my court date, there wasn't a moment I didn't feel terror in my gut. I'd heard all the same horror stories about prison that everyone else has heard, and even though I was a tough cookie, I just didn't see myself as someone who'd fare well there. Although I'd had some hard knocks, mostly of my own design, I didn't have the same set of experiences as someone who'd grown up on the streets. In a church crowd, I would definitely be viewed as "hard," but in the prison crowd, I knew I'd be judged as "soft."

While I knew there were about to be legal and financial consequences, the most brutal one for me, the only one I really cared about, was that I was not allowed to go on tour with "Lisa Daggs and a Touch of Class" because, as a felon, I wasn't allowed to leave the country.

I called Larry Walker, who'd arranged the tour, and begged him to postpone it.

"Sorry, babe," he explained coolly, "They got another front woman and A Touch of Class is going on tour without you."

As I hung up the phone, I felt helpless and abandoned.

Some people say that when you hit bottom, the only way to go is up. But I always took issue with that simple deduction, because I'd hit bottom before and I'd never gone up! In my mind, when you've hit bottom, you can go straight up, or straight sideways. "Straight up" means that you get up, dust yourself off, and start doing right. But—as my many falls had proven—you don't always go *up*. "Straight sideways" means that you can keep sliding further and further in the direction you were already leaning. In my experience, you can be at the bottom, and still somehow find a way to slide even further from becoming the person you were made to be.

To turn it around after you've hit bottom, you have to look up. The Psalmist sings, "I lift up my eyes to the mountains—where does my help come from? My help comes from the LORD, the Maker of heaven and earth" (Psalm 121:1-2). So although I'd been on the bottom before, I'd kept making choices to slide even further from the Lord and from becoming the woman He made me to be.

In my darkest days, I'd heard the Lord whisper, *Are you done? Are you done yet?* And although I was splayed out on the ground, brittle-haired, gray-skinned, with burnt mucus membranes, I wasn't yet done. Although I was rarely snorting coke at this point, I was free-basing, which means I was *smoking* it. As a result, almost every year I was getting bronchitis and pneumonia. Whether I intended to or not, I was slowing killing myself.

I know that my mom and others who cared about me asked themselves, "What's it going to take?"

Experience has taught me that it takes what it takes.

Maybe you have struggled with an eating disorder, and you know what it's like to tell yourself whatever it takes to justify your destructive patterns.

Or maybe your slide into alcoholism was laced with awful moments that felt like you'd hit bottom, only to discover that you could sink even deeper.

Perhaps your addiction to sex or porn began as a "harmless" interest, and before you knew it you'd lost control.

Or maybe your spending that started with a "must-have" outfit snowballed into an uncontrollable and unsustainable pattern of spending.

Like me, you may have had many moments of regret and vowed to live differently, only to find yourself in the pit again.

Beloved, I have some good news.

The *pit* is exactly where God meets us.

Some of us are in pits where someone else has thrown us. Others, like me, are in pits we've dug for ourselves. But whether by the hand of another or by our own, it's not where we belong, and God loves us too much to leave us there.

If you've been there, you know He has the power to scoop you out and put you on solid ground.

And if you're not there yet? If you're not yet ready for rescue? All I can tell you is that you can't avoid God's grace forever. If I learned anything from my dangerous living, it's that some of us can dodge God's goodness for a long time. We can dodge it until we're limping and bleeding and even crawling on gashed knees, but there's nowhere we can get to that is outside of God's reach.

We might get as far as jail.

We might get as far as the hospital.

As long as we are drawing breath, there's nowhere we can go that is beyond God's reach.

And if you've not yet been touched by grace, it's coming for you.

Chapter 11

DECISION

Some lucky addicts and alcoholics skate through their drug and alcohol abuse with few explicit consequences until a single dramatic crisis startles them into sobriety. One alcoholic is caught drinking at work by a supervisor, the light bulb comes on, he realizes he needs help, and he gets it. A woman is high when a school principal calls her to come pick up her sick child, her eyes are opened to her addiction, and she turns her life around. For some, it's because a family member offers an ultimatum. For others, it's an arrest. For others, it may be a long-coming spiritual conviction. However it happens, the person wakes up to the reality of her choices, and turns her life around.

The night of November 12, 1989, as I glanced around at the other broken and bleeding women in my cell, I wanted more than anything to believe that this was the moment my life was going to turn around. That I was going to begin behaving differently. But I'd failed enough times to know this pit might have a false bottom.

Would this time be any different than all the other moments I'd had the opportunity to live differently?

Because my purse had contained drugs I'd packaged in case anyone had hit me up at The Mushroom, I was being charged with possession for sale. That meant I was facing three to five years in prison.

Most of the mornings between my arrest and trial, I woke up pulsing with low-grade terror.

The public defender who'd been assigned to me had given me tips on how to have the very best chances of avoiding prison. He wanted me to continue to go to Narcotics Anonymous meetings. I also needed to go to Alcoholics Anonymous meetings, and walk out with signatures. I needed to get character references from people of good standing. So my closest acquaintances—others who boozed and used—weren't going to cut it. One by one, I gathered references from folks like Pastor Glen Cole, family friends like Theda Oates, and even my mom.

And my very best chance of staying out of prison was to go into rehab.

My mom wanted me to go to a program called Teen Challenge, started by a Christian named David Wilkerson. After seeing pictures in a magazine of teenagers who belonged to a dangerous gang in New York City, Wilkerson moved there and began ministering to them. He founded Times Square Church in New York City, and describes his street ministry in the bestselling book *The Cross and the Switchblade*. A woman named Alpha Henson—the wife of Clyde Henson, who pastored the church we attended when I was growing up—founded the Alpha Henson Home Teen Challenge program in our area. There wasn't room for another girl at that time, but because Lady Henson was my mom's friend, she used her muscle to persuade the program to make room for me. And while my mom was enthused about it, I really didn't want to go there. Although I wanted to change, I still wasn't ready for too much God.

Thankfully a facility called Alpha Oaks Recovery Home had a bed available for me. My mom was willing and able to take me, but I was drumming up every excuse under the sun not to go.

I had to communicate with the members of my band.

I had to be in touch with my boss at work.

I had to organize some things.

I had to do anything that would postpone the humiliation of check-ing into a rehab facility.

My mom allowed me to piddle around for about a day.

Sunday evening I glanced up from a magazine I was reading to see her standing in the doorway of my room.

"We're going tomorrow," she announced firmly.

"Mom," I said, sounding more like a young tween than the twenty-one-year-old I was, "I've got things to do."

Important things, like music magazines.

Without entertaining my protest, my mom simply walked away.

The next morning, I was still in the sweats and T-shirt I'd slept in, dawdling over some oatmeal in the kitchen, when my mom came downstairs. One glance at her slacks, blouse, and jewelry told me she was heading out somewhere.

As serious as I'd ever seen her, she instructed, "Get in the car."

"Mommmmm," I moaned. "I can't go now . . ."

Interrupting my protests, she ordered, "We're going."

Knowing that resistance was futile, I dropped my bowl in the sink, headed to my room to change, walked slowly down that wooden hall-way, and came back fifteen minutes later hauling a duffle bag of essentials.

As we pulled out of the neighborhood and headed toward Alpha Oaks, I drank in each familiar sight as if I *was* being taken to prison.

"How long do I have to stay there?" I asked, sounding a bit petulant.

As the words tumbled out of my mouth, I knew my mom didn't know the answer.

"As long as you need to be there," she replied resolutely.

When we arrived, we were directed to an intake room already filling with a couple other girls, like me, who needed help. Each was accom-panied by her own weary mom. Seated around a long table, a leader from the facility invited us to introduce ourselves. Because we had to name why we were there, it sounded like a corny twelve-step meeting I'd seen on a television show, "Hi, I'm Suzy and I'm an alcoholic."

Totally like a dweeb.

When it was my turn, I said, "I'm Lisa. I'm an addict and I can't drink."

I noticed my mom wince in pain.

It's a little funny that instead of saying I was an alcoholic, I chose to manage the messaging by saying, "I can't drink." Nothing could be further from the truth, In fact, I could drink. And I could drink a lot. But like any good addict or alcoholic worth her margarita salt, I needed to believe that I was different than the other girls in that room. Different than the strung-out users I'd seen in jail. I needed to believe I was better than they were.

After the introductory session, we all said goodbye to our moms.

After giving me a long hug, my mom looked me in the eye and assured me, "You can do this, Lisa. And God will help you."

Although I knew she meant well, I wasn't convinced that either one of those things was true.

Rather than sassing back, I received her blessing, answering, "Thanks, Mom. Love you."

"I love you," she said.

I believed her.

After that handful of scared moms left, we were shown to the rooms where we'd be staying, and told to be in the community meeting room in an hour. Dropping my bag on a chair, I stretched out on the neatly made twin bed in the small room I'd been assigned. Glancing out the window, I noticed two moms still talking together in the parking lot.

We'd been told we'd be participating in a six-week program. Forty-two days felt like an eternity. But I kept reminding myself that those forty-two might spare me at least some of the 1,825 days I could be facing in prison.

That math made forty-two feel a bit more manageable.

Lying on the ugly pea-green bedspread, staring at the ceiling, my mind raced to figure out how I could still go on tour with the band, knowing they were scheduled to leave two weeks later.

Maybe I could be such an amazingly successful client that they'd recognize I wasn't like the others, and release me early.

Realizing that was unlikely, I continued fantasizing.

If I could communicate with someone in my band, maybe I could break out, steal my own passport from my mom's house, hope for a glitch in the system, and leave the country before anyone could catch me.

But I knew that neither the scenario in which I was "really good," or the one in which I was "really bad" were likely. Still, I continued to strategize any possible way I could go on that tour.

Somehow, the very best thing that had happened in my life to date—going on tour and performing for thousands—had collided with the very worst thing to happen in my life. And in the cruel economy of a tattered life, I couldn't figure out a way for the two to co-exist.

When I tired of scheming, I was left with the cold, hard facts: I'd lost everything I'd worked so hard for.

Glancing at the ticking clock over the doorway, I got up and headed to my first meeting. The staff person running it reminded us of what we'd heard earlier with our mothers. The first two weeks of the program were called "blackout."

No visitors.

No phone calls.

No privileges to leave the property.

I felt like I was back in school again. But not the kind some of my peers were enjoying, the carefree college life of attending some classes and being in control of all the other hours. No, this felt more like third grade.

From the moment we woke up to the moment we slept again, our lives were scheduled.

We had to be out of our pajamas and dressed by seven in the morning.

We had to attend morning devotions before breakfast.

We were assigned one day a week on which we could do our personal laundry.

We were responsible for daily chores. (And yes, there was a chore chart, like in third grade.) One week I'd be in charge of setting the tables, the next week taking out the trash, the next week making each meal's entrée, the next week preparing the water and iced tea pitchers for every table, and so one.

And as part of the program, we had to attend ninety meetings in ninety days. On-site we attended forty-two of them.

Because so much of our time was structured, Alpha Oaks also wanted us to have some fun, so on Saturday night we gathered for dances, hosted by a pretty good DJ at a sober AlAnon club.

That's where I learned how to dance sober.

I'm not even going to pretend that I liked it. Frankly, it was completely awkward. Being aware of myself, being aware of others, being aware of what was happening in the room around me was a completely new experience. Honestly, I wasn't a fan. When it came to dancing, doing it high was still my preference.

As days passed, I was forced to release my death grip on the story that I was different than other alcoholics and addicts. That I was better. As I'd sit in meetings, and hear my own story coming out of the mouths of other girls, the narrative of my uniqueness, to which I'd been clinging, began to slip out of my grasp.

At Alpha Oaks, we were all on level ground. No one had walked through the heavy wooden doors of the facility on a winning streak.

An aspiring artist, like me, threw away her dream for the sake of using.

Another woman's marriage had come undone.

One young woman sold her body for drugs.

A girl about my age had stolen from the family that loved her.

A mom was passed out when she was supposed to pick up her child at daycare.

Another one had wrecked her father's car.

All of us began by making small compromises that became bigger ones.

And we all told ourselves stories to convince ourselves that it really "wasn't that bad."

Except that it was.

For a while I'd mentally reassure myself by thinking, "Well at least I didn't do *that*." But as the stories of loss began to pile up, as my eyes were open to the ways that other lives were being destroyed, I recognized the clear connection between addiction and the destruction of lives. As I noticed the ways other lives mirrored my own, I began to recognize how out of control my life had become. How undisciplined. It was as if I was *seeing* for the first time because, with sobriety, the scales were being removed from my eyes.

And although the first moment I set foot in Alpha Oaks, I was counting the minutes until I could leave, it slowly became a place of respite for me. It was a safe place to be as I learned about myself. I didn't have to explain how I was feeling, because twenty other women already knew.

In a very real way, I felt like I'd come home.

In our meetings, I paid special attention to the women who'd been through rehab before. Fearing I could relapse like them, I wanted to learn everything I could from them, from their thinking, about how to get clean and *stay* clean.

When I considered the bleak possibility of unending sobriety, I felt ambivalence. While it was hard to imagine what a substance-free life would look like, I knew exactly what the alternative would look like. I'd either be stumbling back into rehab, like a few of the women at Alpha Oaks, or I'd be dead.

One of the fleeting thoughts that badgered me in these moments was: *Maybe I could learn to drink like a lady.*

In my worst moments, I'd convinced myself—as I'd done for years—that I could manage it.

In my lucid moments, I recognized the voice of the one who lies to my soul.

I'd remember what it was like to go without sleep for ten days.

I'd hear the ominous clink of handcuffs locking behind my back.

I'd taste the stink of vomit in my mouth.

I'd see my gray skin in the bathroom mirror.

I'd smell the urine in back alleys where my friends and I would snort, behind bars.

When I'd see these women walking in for their second or fifth round of rehab, a part of me knew that could easily be me.

After about a week in treatment, it was my turn to share my story with the group. I described how I began using young, and how hard I'd worked to fulfill my dream of being a national recording artist, and how I'd thrown it all away for the sake of using.

"Next week my band leaves for Japan to start the tour without me," I explained, hearing a catch in my own voice that exposed my deep sadness.

After a few moments of silence, a woman in her forties assured me, "Lisa, you are exactly where you need to be."

Understanding my grief, and yet wanting my best, others chimed in.

"This is where you're going to get well."

"This is where you're going to find your help."

"This is where you can start again."

"This is where you'll learn how to do life on life's terms."

Though my disappointment felt like it fueled every cell of my body, their encouragement was feeding me. It was strengthening me. Like a little baby learning to walk, I'd shown up at Alpha Oaks pretty wobbly, but every day I'd take a new step. I'd find the solid ground beneath my feet. I'd get a little stronger.

I was finally learning to walk in the good way.

Eventually I earned the privilege of leaving Alpha Oaks, usually to work my waitressing shift at a restaurant downtown. I'd sign out at the front desk and drive my car to work. When I'd return home, I'd sign back in.

Baby steps.

When I'd earned visiting privileges, my mom would come to see me on Sunday afternoons. She was so *solid* for me during that season, as she'd been throughout my life. It was a comfort to know that when I was released, she would be there for me.

During the eighth week of my stay, my mom asked me to sign out so we could visit her best friend, Theda, who was the mother of one of my good church friends, Judy, who I knew had been clean and sober for several decades.

When Theda opened her front door, she wrapped her arms around me in a big bear hug. While I felt like such a failure, she made me feel like I was the most special and important person on the planet. Stepping inside, I saw Judy, who also embraced me.

It felt so great, so *normal*, to sit around Theda's kitchen table, snacking on crackers and cheese and catching up on everyone's lives.

After an hour or so of gabbing, Theda rose from her seat, pointed toward her bedroom, and suggested, "Let's go sit down in there."

We all rose and followed Theda through her bedroom, and then we were walking down this huge staircase into a room I'd never seen before. The stairs curled into a gentle curve. In the middle of the room was a beautiful brick fire pit, with various pieces of padded furniture circled around it. Had I not known these three women to be mighty women of God, I might have guessed I was being lured into some kind of odd pagan ritual.

As we descended the regal staircase, I started to feel uncomfortable, guessing that something was about to give. Feeling a bit panicked, I feared that whatever was going to happen down there was going to be about me.

What is about to happen?

How can I get out of this?

Knowing my mom and her friends, I suspected what was coming. And I feared it was going to include their powerful prayers.

Everything in me wanted to scramble back up the stairs and yell, "Wait, wait! I'm not ready for this!"

Because my body and mouth weren't willing to cooperate, I dutifully sat down on a brown leather sofa, flanked by Mom, Theda, and Judy.

There was no escape.

Leaning toward me, Judy grabbed my hands.

"Lisa," she began, "you have to let go of your dream."

The words landed in my heart like a load of bricks being dropped from a second-floor window.

With the threat of prison time looming, I knew I needed to surrender my life entirely to God. I wanted to give Him my fear. I wanted to give him my pain. I wanted to give him my addiction. But I wasn't ready to give up my dream.

"You have to let it go," she urged. "If He doesn't have singing for you, you need to let it go now. You need to clear the way so He can do what He wants in your life."

I felt like the wind had been knocked out of me by those bricks.

"God is wanting to pry your fingers off your dream. Let it go, Lisa," she continued.

Everything in me resisted.

Take my fear.

Take my pain.

Even take my alcohol and drugs.

Take everything from me, Lord, but don't take my dream.

When I sang for audiences, I knew that I was being who I was designed to be. Why would God ever want to take that from me, when I was so sure that He had given it to me?

I wanted to sing.

I wanted people to know my name.

I wanted to touch people's lives.

I wanted to make a difference.

I wanted to be big.

As I sat on Theda's couch beside the prayer fire pit, I had no idea that for weeks these ladies had been fervently praying for this day. No wonder a war raged in my flesh.

I knew I needed to rededicate my life to Christ, and I was ready to do it. Although Alpha Oaks pointed participants toward a higher power, it was not an explicitly Christian program. But it did emphasize spiritual wellness and incorporate the traditions and principles, such as daily prayer readings, that I recognized from Christianity. When the program's liturgy referenced "God as I understand him," my spirit warmed, and I knew, "Oh, I know who He is!" He was Jesus. It had become clear to me that I couldn't do life on my own, and I needed God's help.

I was cool with God taking almost everything from me, but not my music.

There were several minutes of silence as I considered what Judy was asking of me. While I'd begun to imagine what a life of sobriety might look like, I still couldn't picture what life would look like if I wasn't hustling after my dream.

And yet, like every addict or alcoholic who comes to the end of her rope, I was out of options. I'd tried living life on my terms, and had made a mess of it. In the power of my own strength I'd earned charges for a reckless DUI before I was twenty-one, a DUI, a second DUI with possession, and possession for sale. With no more excuses, and trusting that somehow these women who knew and loved God also knew and loved me, I finally gave up. Resistance sapped, wilting on the inside, I was done.

Feeling the hands of those three mighty women upon me, I negotiated with the Almighty in my heart.

God, if this is what You're asking, then I'm willing to do it. I'm confused. I'm heartbroken. I'm disappointed. I don't understand. But in this moment, I'm going to trust You beyond what I can understand. Help me to pry my fingers off my dream. Have Your way in my life. I'm choosing to trust You.

When we finished praying, I felt exhausted. But also, against all reason, I felt *free.*

What I didn't understand in that moment, and what I wouldn't truly understand for years, is that in those holy moments, the foundation of the new life God had for me was being built. It wasn't a life I could have predicted. It certainly wasn't one I'd chosen. But even in my confusion, I had a tiny seed of confidence that God was going to rebuild my life.

I didn't know how.

I didn't know when.

I didn't know anything.

I just reached out for God's hand, and felt His sure steady grip on mine.

Today, whenever I close my eyes and picture that day, I see my mom, Judy, and Theda present, ushering me into God's presence. And then, in my spirit, I see them leaning out of the way so I could meet God, hand-to-hand.

And, through tears of grief and joy, I did.

Whatever You have for me, Lord, I'm in all the way.

One morning that week after I prayed with that mighty triumvirate of women, I woke up and knew my band was at the airport, heading out tour as a group that no longer had my name on it. And yet as crushed as I was not to be with them, and as terrified as I was of the future that lay ahead of me, I also noticed a new sense of peace. When I had opened my hands to release my dream, it was as if something that had been *holding me* was also released.

I was free.

I wonder what you might be clutching in your hands today.

Maybe, like me, it's a dream of a beautiful future you've envisioned.

Maybe it is literally a Scotch bottle. A pipe. A bottle of prescription pills.

It could be an unhealed wound from the past.

It might be something that no one else sees except for you and God.

It might be an unhealthy someone you don't think you can live without.

Close your eyes and ask God to show you your hands, and what they might be clinging to.

What do you see?

You might see something beautiful, like the image of a hoped-for child. Or you might see something that is clearly destructive, like an abusive relationship. It doesn't matter what it is, because as long as you're gripping it, you can't receive the good God has for you.

Whatever it is, ask God to help you let it go. Visualize yourself at the foot of the cross, releasing whatever you're clutching, to Jesus. See your hands opening, and see Him receiving your offering.

Notice how you feel.

Notice what is different inside you.

And over the next days and months, I also want you to notice how God is filling up those open hands. Precious one, even though you may not be able to see it yet, He has so much more for you than you can imagine.

Trust me.

Chapter 12

COMING TO JESUS

Sixty days after I arrived, I left Alpha Oaks. As I got into my mom's car to drive to my court date, I had no idea what the future held for me. Although I still lived with the palpable terror of the impending jail time I expected, I did feel like I had the tools to stay clean and sober. One day at a time.

The day my case went to court, I woke up feeling nauseous and terrified. I felt crushed by the very real possibility that I wouldn't be coming home to my mom's house that night, and maybe even for as long as five years. When my mom and I met up in the courthouse that morning, I noticed that we'd both made an effort to look our best. She wore a tasteful navy dress suit, and I wore khaki slacks, a black blazer, and a silk champagne-colored blouse. I'd pulled my long blonde hair back into a very tame pony-tail. Taking one last peek in the hallway mirror before we headed out the door, I decided I did not look like a dangerous addict at all. I hoped the judge would agree.

At the end of the day, when my mom and I fell into a booth at a local burger joint, we were both dumbfounded by what had unfolded in court.

I was given four years formal probation.

I was assigned two hundred hours of community service.

I was given a twelve-thousand-dollar fine, which, almost to the penny, was all of the money I had saved in the bank from the money I made dealing.

I wasn't sentenced to a single day in prison.

Some called it a technicality in the court system.

I call it a miracle. And I can only attribute the outcome to God's benevolent mercy that I most certainly did not deserve.

Still, the road ahead was a long one. With a felony on my record, I needed to complete my service hours and find a job. I also needed to grow in my faith. Graciously, my former church, Capital Christian Center, welcomed me to complete my service hours there, through an alternative sentencing program.

After parking my car in the sprawling but near-empty weekday parking lot of the six-thousand-member church and breathing a prayer for grace, I grabbed my sack lunch, shoved it in my purse, and walked toward the front door. When I'd been active there as a teen, I felt cared for by the members and staff I knew. And even though I hadn't yet given my life entirely to God at that point, though I still clung fiercely to my habits and plans, I knew I was loved by God. When I'd left six and a half years earlier to pursue my big dreams, I hadn't found another church in Nashville. Although I went to church on occasion, I never sought out a place where I could grow and use my gifts.

As I stepped from the parking lot onto the paved walkway to the church's front door, I couldn't help but think of the story Jesus tells of the son who left his father's home in search of something better. I don't know if he had a dream of making it big, like I did. Jesus doesn't say. What I do know is that he grabbed his share of his father's money, took off for a distant country, and spent it on wild living. And let me tell you, between the racy relationships, the booze, the drugs, the fines, and the court fees, life can get pretty pricy. That's why, when he'd blown through all he had, he came groveling back to his dad, planning to ask for the job of a servant.

Pulling open one of the massive front doors of the church, I felt like I knew a little bit about what that party boy had felt when he got to his childhood home. Thankfully, I hadn't ripped off the church like he'd done to his dad, but it was no secret that I'd left home, messed up, and had come back with my tail between my legs.

Stepping into the beautifully appointed lobby of the new building, I headed toward the staff offices. Although I'd wanted to quietly check in with the receptionist and get right to work, Pastor Donny Burleson, who was heading toward his office, saw me and his face lit up.

"Lisa!" he bellowed. "It's so great to see you. I'm glad you'll be with us."

It was my first taste of much grace I'd receive at Capital, both as a volunteer and also as a member. And to this day, when I think of the gracious faces of both Pastor Donny and Senior Pastor Glen Cole, I think I got the tiniest glimpse of what that prodigal son, who Jesus described, saw on his father's face.

When I quietly gave my name and reason for being there to the receptionist, she sent me to meet one of the pastors, Ray Guinta. Ray had spearheaded the alternative sentencing community service program at the church, welcoming folks like me—who I used to think were nothing like me! Some of the community service workers had grown up in church, like me, but many had never set foot in a house of worship. But any who were assigned to Capital were welcomed and known and loved like I was. It was one of many beautiful ministries of that church. On that first day I worked alongside Ray's assistant, organizing closets and storage rooms. After that, I basically did anything that needed to be done.

It took me about five weeks of full-time work to complete my court-required hours. Knowing I needed paying employment, the church offered me a position as the assistant to the church administrator's assistant. Pretty impressive, huh? What it looks like to be at the bottom of the secretary ladder is that everything the other assistants hadn't been able to get done—needing an answer about this building issue, or a call back from that colleague, or a bill from that plumber—landed on my little desk. The work was incredibly tedious. But it was work. And I was grateful.

Some folks whose lives have gone up in a ball of fire—whether they're coming off the streets, landing at home after rehab, or being released from prison—have no place to go other than back to the streets. They have no people other than the ones who were using with them. As you might imagine, being in the same old places with the same old people makes the task of rebuilding a life even more difficult.

But, thanks be to God, I had landed in a safe place. I lived at home with my mom, who prayed for me and supported me. Every day I worked in an environment where people wanted to see me succeed. No one at Capital Christian Center treated me like the humbled sinner I was. In fact Pastor Glen and his wife MaryAnn called me their "trophy of grace." Isn't that beautiful? As a staff, we shared devotions every day. We prayed together. It was an amazing place to land while God loved me back to life. I had even come to have a sense of peace about my decision to release my death grip on my dreams of becoming a performer. I knew that my life was in *God's* hands.

One Sunday morning in worship, I heard that a traveling evangelist named Lowell Lundstrom would be offering a concert the following weekend. Lowell and his wife Connie had been performing on the road, sharing the Gospel for years. And Lowell's brother Larry had a matching tour bus! Lowell had forty records and the family had been ministering to audiences for decades. Saturday night I attended the concert with my mom, and it was amazing. On the ride home I felt fully alive in a way I hadn't for a long time.

Excited to hear them again on Sunday morning, I showed up early to get a front-row seat. Once again, spiritual energy pulsed through my veins as they performed. I didn't feel envious, like I might have if a young woman my age had been ministering up front. Instead, I just felt a sense of fullness. My spirit resonated with what they were about and I was able to celebrate what God was doing through them. Though I didn't recognize it at the time, that was part of the good growth the Lord was doing in me.

After worship, the Lundstrom family and crew shared lunch with Capital's pastoral staff before heading out. Their next concert was scheduled for the following evening in Vacaville, which was about forty-five minutes away. Over dessert, they chatted about their families. Lowell and his wife Connie were thrilled that their daughter was expecting her first child.

"I am trying to find a way to go be with her when the baby's born," Connie explained.

As she spoke, MaryAnn got an idea.

"Did you see that little girl sitting on the front row?" she asked.

There's really no reason they should have, with such a full audience, but I really had been getting my praise on, so there's a chance they may have noticed.

MaryAnn continued, "Well, she's an alto, and she's got a *great* voice."

Connie and Lowell glanced at each other, raising their eyebrows at the possibility.

"Well," Lowell began, still thinking it over, "why don't you have her meet us before tomorrow's show in Vacaville?"

Grinning, MaryAnn promised, "She'll be there!"

Sunday afternoon I was piddling around the kitchen when the phone rang. When MaryAnn identified herself, she sounded downright giddy, as if she was bursting to share some incredible news. As the words poured out of her, it slowly began to dawn on me what she was saying.

Obviously, the only appropriate response to such news is to scream.

In seconds, my mom came running from her bedroom.

"Lisa, what is it?! Are you alright?" she called out before even reaching the kitchen. Seeing me holding the phone, she added, "Is everyone else alright?"

Torn between learning more from MaryAnn and telling my mom, I spilled out a few words my mom didn't understand, then finished my conversation with MaryAnn, thanked her, and hung up.

"MOM!" I hollered, even though she was standing six feet away. "The Lundstroms want me to audition!!!"

Because I'd talked about little else besides the Lundstroms since the previous evening, my mom also had to take a moment to process the information.

"Audition for what?" she asked.

"Lowell's wife Connie wants to take a break from the tour, when her grandchild is born, and they need an alto!"

My mom, understanding immediately what this meant to me, queried, "So when do you audition?"

"Tomorrow! In Vacaville!"

When we both finished dancing around the kitchen, I went up to my room to pore over songs and decide which one to prepare for my big shot.

The next day I asked to leave work early, to make sure I got to the church in Vacaville on time. Before leaving my job at Capital Christian Center, I changed into a blouse and skirt and fixed my hair and makeup. Peeking in the mirror of the church's bathroom, I knew I wasn't going to be judged on my appearance, but I wanted everything to be perfect. Arriving an hour before I was to meet them, I sang and prayed in the parking lot before heading in to the church, just as the band was finishing the sound checks.

I explained my situation to a security guard, who let me approach the stage.

"Excuse me," I said a bit timidly, "Mr. Lundstrom, I'm Lisa Daggs, from Capital Christian Center, and I was told I could meet you here for an audition."

Reaching down to shake my hand, he said, "Nice to meet you, Lisa. Are you available for the next several months?"

Knowing I had the full support of the staff at church I confirmed, "Yes, sir. I can be!"

"Lisa," he said, pointing to a gentleman sitting in the front of the sanctuary, "talk to our manager, David Day Jr., and he can give you the details about the rest of the tour."

Confused, I thanked him and went to speak to the road manager. He already seemed to be looped in, and told me how I could stay in contact with him about when I'd begin. That's right, I never auditioned! Less than a year after I'd given God my dreams, truly letting them go, I was heading out on tour. Without auditioning.

Only. God.

Chapter 13

GOD'S DREAM FOR ME BEGINS

Two months later, just before the Lundstrom's grandchild was due, I joined the tour as the new kid on the block. We traveled all over the country doing shows, and I had the opportunity to share my testimony with audiences at those events, usually singing "Picking up the Pieces" by the Archers.

Although I'd had plenty of experience singing in casinos, bars and clubs, I was now being given the chance to perform *and* testify to God's goodness. Daily, I had a sense that I was doing exactly what I was made for. I'd been clean for six months when we left, and I celebrated my first anniversary of sobriety on that tour. I was practicing what it meant both to live clean and as a Christian, using the twelve-step tools I'd been given: "Think, think, think," "Let go and let God," and "But for the grace of God go I." And it was a gift to be with Lowell and Connie, who were sold out to God, and to watch how they lived their lives. Most importantly, perhaps, I knew that they loved me.

It wasn't always easy. I wish I could say I was in a safe Christian bubble that protected me from temptation during the tour, but that's just not the case. Even in Christian circles, the enemy can creep in. Graciously, God kept me from descending down that slippery slope back into sin.

In each city where we visited on a weekend, we would host a crusade at a community center or under an open-air tent on Sunday nights. So on Sunday mornings Lowell would send four of us to different local churches where we'd perform a song and then invite the congregation to bring an unbelieving friend to the Sunday night event where he or she would have the opportunity to meet Christ. As a result, these shows, designed to minister to both believers and unbelievers, were usually packed. It was thrilling to see the fruit God was producing as person after person, in city after city, came to know and trust Jesus Christ.

While skeptics might call the system a mechanically orchestrated production, I saw firsthand the passion that Lowell Lundstrom had for those who were lost to know the Lord. Lowell was an avid reader, and the first thing he'd do when we stopped in each city was to grab the local newspaper to see what was happening there. If one of us would knock on his door, we'd see newspapers open all over the room! So although he couldn't know every person at each event, he did know something of what each community was celebrating or grieving. He knew the teams. He knew the economy. He knew the tragedies. Each night he trusted the Holy Spirit to move in human hearts, but he also did his part.

Though I couldn't yet see how God would one day use the experience in my life, as I watched Lowell and Connie I was learning both the creative and business side of ministry. Lowell could make anything into a song. He'd just start singing, and we'd all wait to see what would come out of his mouth. Sometimes it would be, "You can't get to Heaven with a U-Haul trailer!" He had a knack for putting things into song, and I was paying attention. I learned from Lowell that great songs aren't written, they're *rewritten.* So I started writing and honing my own songs. Far less glamorous was that I was learning about running a ministry, from scheduling gigs to sending bulk newsletter mailings.

On the road we'd often have media opportunities to promote the local shows. In Concord, about ninety minutes outside Sacramento, I was interviewed on a Christian television station that was a satellite of the popular PTL Network. I wasn't always the featured guest for these media gigs, but the host of *Great Life Today* was my former youth pastor, Rich Wilkerson, who'd known me since I was a girl. We had a great conversation, I prayed that someone struggling, who might have just been flipping through channels, would pause and come to know God's abundant grace and mercy. I knew there were many others like me who'd been raised in the church, had chosen to walk away and do their own thing, and then had been wooed back to the One Who never let them go.

"Rich," I marveled, reflecting on that journey, "God is so different this time."

And while I know he knew what I meant, he replied, "Lisa, did you ever think it's *you* who's different now?"

On-air, I nodded thoughtfully as I processed his comment. And I continued to chew on those words that had landed deep in my soul. Because he was right. God is unchanging. For a host of reasons, I was the one who chose to numb the pain inside me with drugs and alcohol. I had more confidence in their power to save than I did in God's power to meet my needs and satisfy my thirst. I believe I could just as easily ended up in the grave as in rehab, but in God's mercy I lived. Perhaps because of the way I'm made, because of who I am, I had to be completely broken before I was willing to give God permission to put me back together. To live according to his design. To be redeemed. Rich was right. That was on me.

When the tour got to Sisseton, South Dakota, I had the opportunity to record my first record with the group. I'd been clean and sober for six months, and I sang "Picking up the Pieces of My Life." That, the story of someone being pulled out of the gutter by God, was a new dimension to the Lundstroms' ministry.

When we performed in Sullivan, Illinois, my aunt Fran came to our concert after hearing my story for the first time on *Great Life Today*. When she hugged me after the show, I was able to see the way my broken pieces were not only touching the lives of strangers, but could even impact people who'd really known me for years. Day after day, week after week, I marveled at God's grace. Not only had He redeemed me, which was more than enough, but He'd also given me the privilege of making His grace known. Until then, the biggest dream I'd had for my life had been the Department of Defense tour. But as I was discovering God's dream for me, I was learning it wasn't about being *big*, it was about being *small*—by sharing my mistakes with perfect strangers to magnify what God had done in my life.

Months earlier, when my life was in shambles, I sat in a holy fire pit prayer room at Theda's house, and gave everything to God. At the time I didn't understand why God would ask me to hand over my dream of singing, but I trusted His ministry to me through those three women enough to do it. I trusted God enough to do it. Even though I couldn't fathom the mystery of God's ways, what I did know was that He loved me and that He was good.

I expect that if you've been in the darkness, and God has asked you to trust Him for what you couldn't see, you know how scary it is to let go of that idol you've clung to. And while I know the word "idol" can conjure up visions of little wooden statues worshipped in foreign cultures, it's really anything you trust to provide or meet your needs more than God. For me that was my dogged pursuit of my dream. It was my hustle. For you it might be a fertility specialist. Or an online dating app. Or a lottery ticket.

What I really want you to hear is that, beyond what you can see, God is able to make a way where it seems like there's no way. Never in my wildest dreams could I have orchestrated what had unfolded in my life that year, by God's good design. And it's possible—no, probable!—that you can't predict how God will answer the deep prayers and yearnings of your own heart. I had tried everything I knew how to do, contacted every connection, leveraged every network, hustled to get gigs, rehearsed and then rehearsed some more, but none of efforts were what finally opened the door of opportunity for me.

God was.

Friend, there is nothing that God desires more than for you to become the person you were designed to be. In fact, I suspect His plan is already unfolding in your life in ways you may not yet have eyes to see. And your part in the beautiful execution of that master plan is to keep your eyes on the Master planner and live in response to Him. In the recovery community, we are encouraged to do "the next right thing." When you don't know what to do, do the next right thing, and in time you'll discover God's good plan for your life that you never could have orchestrated for yourself.

After our gigs in the United States, the tour was scheduled to perform in several Canadian cities. After our final domestic gig for this tour, in Grand Forks, North Dakota, we were lined up to cross the border into Winnepeg, Manitoba. For reasons we weren't privy to, border-patrol agents asked the bus to pull over. After ordering everyone onboard to get off, they split us up into separate interview rooms to question us.

As I sat down face-to-face with an agent across a small metal table, my heart began to beat faster. I didn't know much about international law, but I suddenly wondered if my past was going to pose a problem.

After a few basic identifying queries, the agent asked me, "Have you ever been arrested for anything?"

In the twinkling of an eye, I had to make a decision about whether or not I'd tell them the truth. If I did tell the truth, I feared they'd not let me cross the border. Then I reasoned, maybe if I was completely transparent, they would honor the fact that I'd told them truth by letting me enter. If I lied, I not only jeopardized the credibility of the Lundstrom family, I feared I might face other charges if the truth did come out. Knowing in my gut what was right, I decided to tell the truth.

Taking a deep breath and turning on the charm, I announced, "Get your pen and paper ready, because I've got a list for you!"

Quick.

Honest.

Funny.

Transparent.

I felt like my answer met all the criteria for a win.

The somber border agent saw it differently.

With an undisguised look of disgust for the American felon, he hissed, "We don't want your kind here."

I was crushed. With no other option, the band got a hotel room for me. I was detained while the tour continued.

Chapter 14

ON A ROAD CALLED GRACE

My legal troubles at the Canadian border taught me an import-ant lesson: although the Lord forgives, people aren't always as quick to do the same! Yet through some legal advocacy, an attorney Lowell contacted helped me get a visitation pass to stay in Canada for the final twelve days of the tour. The snafu reminded me that when we sin, there will still be consequences for our actions.

After eight months, I flew home from that tour date feeling full and grateful for the opportunity I'd been given. Back home at my mom's, with the new recording I'd made at Lowell and Con-nie's studio, I began crafting a new bio and getting new headshots in the hopes of opening the doors for my own music ministry.

Not long after I returned, I attended a worship conference in San Jose, where I had an amazing experience and learned so much about leading others into the heart of God. I'd been home only a few min-utes when I'd received a phone call that shook me to the core.

My mom, who'd come to the kitchen to see who'd called, watched me as I spoke to the stranger.

". . . okay, thank you for calling," I said halfheartedly.

After setting the phone receiver back in its cradle, I sat in dazed silence.

"What is it?" my mom asked, with concern in her voice.

"That was the hospital in Concord," I told her. "Dad's had a stroke."

"Lisa, I'm so sorry," she cooed.

Though they'd been divorced for more than a decade, she had always been kind to the man whose broken promises had made her life pretty difficult at times.

She asked, "Do your brothers know?"

"Ummm . . ." I began, still in a bit of a daze, "I think I was the first person they contacted. I can let Larry and Tim know."

My mom intuited that I might be conflicted about the situation, and she was right. She'd known for years that I had always wanted more of my dad than was ever available to me. Both as a girl and as a young woman.

"Lisa," she asked gently, "how are you doing?"

I was touched by the care I heard in her voice.

"I don't know," I answered honestly. "I'm not sure what to think or do."

"Would you like me to go with you to the hospital?"

"Yeah," I answered with relief, "that would be great, Mom. Thank you."

It didn't surprise me one bit that she was willing to show up for the man who'd left her. After reflecting on what was happening a bit more, I knew intuitively what I needed to do.

"Dad has never been there for me," I said, "but I'm gonna be there for him."

All I can say is that *had* to have been the Lord. The tables had suddenly turned: the one who was strong but couldn't find time for me when I was vulnerable was now weak, and I was faced with the choice of whether or not to show up for him. In my own strength, I wouldn't have mustered the will to be gracious to my father. But fueled by the Lord's kindness, I was able to show up for him when he needed me most.

After his stroke, my dad entered a local rehab facility and continued to improve, getting stronger every day. But just before he was to be discharged four months later, he suffered a second stroke that really set him back.

When my dad realized he was no longer able to take care of himself at home, he checked himself into the VA home in Yountville. Because he couldn't pack up his apartment himself, I offered to do it. A guy friend I'd met in AA and I packed everything my dad owned into cardboard boxes and took them to a storage unit. While we were extracting shoes and boxes and ties and blazers from my dad's closet, I accidentally unearthed a stash of cocaine safely tucked away in a Christmas tin. I wasn't tempted to use it in that moment, but there were no guarantees that a few weeks later I wouldn't be ready to claw open the padlock on the outside of the storage unit. Just to be on the safe side, the coke was the first thing I put into the outside storage locker. Tucking the red-and-green tin into the far back right corner of the dismal dark unit, my friend and I started stacking furniture, building box towers, and filling every crack with bags of extra clothes until the unit was full. If I was ever tempted to get those drugs, I'd have to unpack every single item we'd worked so hard to wedge in there. The memory of the grueling day we'd spent packing and lifting and transporting and delivering was going to make the temptation very minimal.

In those early months, I had no idea where my relationship with an increasingly weak and physically disabled father was headed. But I remained steadfast in my conviction that I was called to be there for him.

I was also continuing to work on my own healing as I discovered what it looked like to live sober. As I worked through the twelve steps, I made a list of everyone against whom I was holding resentments, and the cause of each one. As part of that process, I was responsible for naming the part I'd played in the broken relationship. Had I been selfish? Insecure? Dishonest?

I had a sponsor named Barbara Battersby who helped me navigate the twelve steps. She walked with me as I began to explore, for the first time, the ways a father is supposed to love his baby girl. While that was painful, I also learned that we have no control over other human beings. What I *could* do was to notice my part in the broken relationship, and ask for forgiveness. Even if the other person never acknowledges their part, I was finding out that I'm not responsible for cleaning that side of the street. In the program, this is known as the Fourth Step Inventory.

Though I'd borne the heavy weight of disappointment and rejection for years, I'd never told my dad I didn't feel loved. One Saturday I made a special visit to the VA home in Yountville to speak the truth I prayed he would be able to hear. But I knew that whether he received it or not, I had to do my part by sharing it.

I'd called ahead to let my dad know I was coming, and felt really anxious as I sat down beside him.

"Dad," I began, with a quiver of fear in my voice, "I'm sorry I held a resentment against you. Because when I was a girl and you came home at night, I didn't feel loved. I need to apologize that I've been holding onto that resentment toward you for not treating me like your baby girl. I'm sorry I kept this from you, and held you responsible."

Even though I knew my dad wasn't completely emotionally healthy himself, he understood this was part of my healing process, and he received my words. Although I'd been to enough meetings to hear stories of these encounters going poorly, I dared to hope that something in him would be unlocked and he would shower me with the affection I'd yearned for so long. But that night was not the night. On my drive back home, I thanked God for giving me the courage to do my work and prayed that somehow something would eventually change between us.

When I wasn't singing, either at my own gigs or on the Capital Christian Center's singles worship team, I'd begun writing songs in my bedroom. It was such a holy time of prayer and gratitude for all the Lord had done for me, as I'd welcome the Holy Spirit to give me whatever words I was to share with others. Day after day, I felt like a vessel through which God's Spirit was flowing. Even though the tour had ended, I wasn't finished telling the world all that God had done for me. After all, I'd made a promise. Two of the songs that flowed out of my heart and mind, my fingers and voice, during that season were "My House" and "I Wanna Thank You."

After I'd chatted with Rich Wilkerson on the *Great Life Live* television show in Concord, I had been introduced to a talent scout named Mitch Solarek who took a genuine interest in me and my work. Mitch had been dabbling in management and took me under his wing. As a result, I'd get little opportunities here and there, like recording a jingle for Raley's supermarket. And while being in the recording studio for that little gig felt like home, I believed the Lord was on the edge of rewarding me in His timing. A contest was about to come to Sacramento.

Does any of this sound a little familiar? Getting opportunities to perform with the hope of being offered a *big* opportunity? So how was my life any different than the one I'd struggled so hard to release back to God? It was different because this time was a much different hustle: not aggressive, but surrendered. Before I met Christ in a transforming way, I'd been seeking out any opportunity to be seen and heard. So from the outside, this season didn't look so different. I was writing music, I was having a few opportunities to record, and if I was invited to perform, I said yes. On the outside, the two periods would have looked somewhat similar.

What was different was *me*.

I was clean and sober. That alone was a seismic shift.

I was walking with the Lord.

I didn't *need* to succeed.

Did I *want* to succeed? Sure! But while I'd once been driven by the desire to see my name on marquees and album covers, my heart had changed. I wanted to honor the Lord with the gifts He'd given, and was purposing to be faithful to do that. And this time I was surrounded by a community, at church and at home, who were helping to keep me grounded. I was singing and sharing my testimony at various church events, and asking those pastors for references. Slowly, my booking schedule was growing.

In the spring of 1990, Voice of the 90s held a competition downtown Sacramento at the Crest Theater. Opened in 1912 as a vaudeville palace, it was subsequently renovated, maintaining all the historic décor and appointments. There I would be competing against about two dozen other hopefuls who were as hungry for their own big break as I was. It was almost like I'd been training for this moment for years. All the rehearsals, the countless gigs in clubs, singing in churches, and of course the Lundstrom tour, had all prepared me for what I'd need to do onstage at the Crest.

On the night of the show, I carried a duffle bag in one hand and a garment bag over my shoulder. After staking out a little spot backstage, I looked in the mirror to confirm that nothing had smeared or smudged, wrinkled or fallen, since I'd last checked at home. My permed blonde hair fell below my shoulders in a cascade of tousled curls. The yoke of my tailored black blazer was trimmed with silver piping and embellished with a beautiful pattern of large and small rhinestones that glimmered under stage lights. Over black leggings, my tight black suede boots climbed to my knees. Leaning into the mirror, I checked my makeup, wiping the tiniest speck of mascara off my cheek.

I'd met the other contestants at a run-through the day before. I greeted a few of them and then closed my door to quiet my heart and mind before the show. Lifting a brief silent prayer in my heart, I told God, "Father, I don't deserve anything more from You. You have been so gracious to me. So not my will, but yours."

Peeking from behind the stage curtain, I saw my mom in the fourth-row seat I'd reserved for her. My dad, increasingly feeble, wasn't there. Nor did I expect he would have been if he'd been in good health. Our relationship remained complicated.

I listened from backstage as the first seven singers performed. A few sang songs they'd written. Others sang popular tunes. Genres ranged from pop to rock to country to jazz. As in the other events in which I'd competed, I wanted each one to have the experience of knowing they'd done their very best. But of course I also wanted to win! In the best-case scenario, both would be true.

I was the eighth performer. Poised backstage, filled with anticipation, I waited for the host to announce, "Lisa Daggs." As the hyped crowd welcomed me, I stepped up to the microphone at center stage. Though near-blind from the stage lights, I'd heard and could sense that every seat in the house was filled.

After a few bars, I joined the recorded background music track to sing a song I'd recently composed called "My House." Driven by a haunting melody, the lyrics describe one person being welcomed into the home of another. As the song unfolds, it becomes apparent that the visitor wants to be changed. The host invites the guest to discover the genuine grace and transforming love of Christ. Secure, I executed each word and note as I'd planned. As I finished and returned the microphone to its stand, the crowd erupted in applause. Offering a slight bow of gratitude, noticing the front-row judges beginning to scribble notes and scores, I waved to the audience and left the stage.

Heart racing, receiving kind words from the other performers backstage, I felt confident about what I'd done. After everyone had performed, there was a brief intermission for the judges to tally their scores before announcing the ten finalists, who would be given the opportunity to perform a second song. From those performances, the judges would choose two contestants to go head-to-head in the final round of the competition.

We had been asked to remain backstage during the break. I had already changed outfits in the hope I'd be invited to perform a second song and was drinking water when I noticed some activity at the backstage entrance. One of the production assistants, wearing a headset and holding a clipboard, appeared to be trying to keep someone from coming in. Stepping a bit closer, I saw that it was my mom! Worried something might be wrong, I rushed to the door.

I heard her explaining in her most polite voice, "I just have to get her a message."

"Hey," I explained to the earnest assistant, "She's my mom. Can you just give us a minute?"

Reluctantly, he allowed her to pass, and we stepped to the side to talk.

"Lisa," she said, with excitement in her eyes, "I have a word for you."

In case you don't have a prophetic praying mother of your own, I can explain. For years, my faithful mom had received prophetic words from God, and she'd always been a faithful steward of them. Humbly, she'd offer me or one of my brothers—or at times, perfect strangers—whatever word or warning or promise God had laid on her heart. In the days when I was far from the Lord, my response was most typically, "Yeah, Mom, whatever." But again and again, as I noticed what she had foretold came to pass, I began to value the revelations she shared. That she'd been given a word during this pivotal moment in my career felt significant. I was all ears.

Slowly, as if listening to God saying them again, she spoke the words He had given her, "No man shall stand before you."

As she spoke, I was convicted that these words had come directly from God. Squeezing my mom, I sent her back to her seat and waited to hear the judge's decision.

When the judges read their choices for the top ten finalists, my name was among them. I would be the third performer in Round Two.

For my second number, I'd chosen a very different song from the first round to showcase my versatility as a performer. To ensure the contrast wasn't overlooked, I'd chosen a different kind of outfit, too. Rather than the sassy black garb of the previous round, this time I wore a cream-colored Nolan Miller suit with pearl-trimmed pockets, collar, and cuffs. I donned cream leather pumps, and my hair was tucked up in a roll, with some wisps hanging down past my ornate pearl earrings as I played the keyboard.

When my name was announced a second time, I stepped onto stage in my new sophisticated look. As my music began, I sang a power ballad called "Your Love Stays With Me." As I finished, the crowd again confirmed the sense of accomplishment I felt, performing as well as I'd intended.

After all ten finalists had performed, the judges prepared to announce the winner. Lined up along the front of the stage, ten across, we all grabbed hands and waited. The judges began by announcing the tenth-place finalist, then ninth, and so on.

When there were just four of us left, I dared to hope I might actually take it all.

Moments later, two of us were on stage.

I stood beside a contestant named Scott Abbott, a friend of mine who used a wheelchair. Anxious and excited, we held hands, waiting for the judges' final decision.

"And the winner of our 1990 Voice of the 90s Competition is . . ."

They kept us hanging in brutally painful silence.

"Lisa Daggs!"

I gave Scott a hug and pressed my hands to my face. The moment felt surreal. Bowing and nodding to each of the judges, I mouthed the words "thank you." I knew my mom was in the fourth row, and I saw her beaming and bouncing!

In the midst of the chaos, the words from the Lord she had delivered rang in my ears. *No man shall stand before you.*

Part of my prize was the opportunity to record with Pakaderm Records, owned by John and Dino Elefante, in Los Angeles. Dino was one of the judges; John, his brother, had played guitar and sung for the rock band Kansas.

In 1990, many in the music industry were saying Christian country was going to be the next big thing. When I got my opportunity to record, Mitch invited Greg Long to join. Greg had been one of the lead singers in the band on the Lundstrom tour, and like me, had been working to break into the industry. Pakaderm, which was funded by Word Records, ended up signing me and Greg on the same day.

Not a day went by that I *didn't* thank God for what He'd done for me.

Touring with the Lundstroms had been the opportunity I needed to be seen and heard as part of a group. More importantly, being selected to join them reminded me the Lord had not forgotten me. And The Voice of the 90's was the launch I needed to step into the solo career I'd always dreamed about. After getting the opportunity to record, my first national release was called "Angel in Your Eyes." My first single to climb the charts to Number One was a song that shares my testimony, called "I Wanna Thank You."

The Lord did that.

When my songs started playing on the radio, old friends and folks from church would congratulate me and say how proud they were of me. And while I appreciated the praise, I was crystal clear about Who deserved it. I knew I'd scrambled after success with my own strength, and always come up empty-handed. It wasn't until I let go that God opened the doors that allowed me to succeed. So although I'd done my part by training my voice, rehearsing, and saying "yes" when doors opened, I knew that it was God Who'd been the Giver of all good gifts in my life.

When we taste success—whether at work or at home or at church, whether measured by trophies or accolades or dollars in the bank—it can be tempting to believe that we *earned* it. In fact, it's *natural* to believe we earned it. But James 1:17 asserts that "every good and perfect gift is from above, coming down from the Father of the heavenly lights, who does not change like shifting shadows." You've probably seen well-heeled actors and singers and other performers stepping behind a microphone at awards ceremonies to offer their acceptance speeches. Those who are people of faith will often point to the heavens or find some other way to acknowledge God's role in their success. I now count myself among those who would have little to show for their efforts were it not for God's gracious intervention.

What has God done in your life that you could not have done for yourself? Maybe the Lord gave you the spouse you prayed for. Or the child you'd held in your heart. Perhaps it was a personal goal or a professional accomplishment. Maybe God equipped you with what you needed to make it through college or graduate school. Or it could be that God made a way to put food on the table, pay for your education, or put a down payment on a house when you saw no way. When we succeed, the world is quick to insist that we have pulled ourselves up by our bootstraps. We've grabbed the brass ring. We've lived the American dream. Since God pulled me out of the pit, transforming my life into something much more beautiful than I could have orchestrated on my own, there is no question in my mind Who is to be thanked and praised for the gifts I've been given.

After winning Voice of the 90s, doors began to open for me. Professionally, I was gaining momentum. But part of my heart longed to share life with a man who loved me and loved God. I'd dated plenty of men who were clearly *not* part of God's plan for me, but I was hungry to meet the one who was.

Chapter 15

A LOVE STORY

"Is this seat taken?"

The fine young man who'd caught my attention as he walked up the center aisle at Capital Christian Center wasn't speaking to me, but I was all ears. All eyes. All interested.

Our singles group had just sung a few songs, and we were sitting down to listen to one of the group's leaders who was climbing the stairs to the stage to address us. That's when I noticed this guy with long curly black hair slide into a seat a couple rows ahead of me. I hadn't seen him before at church, but I watched him bop into the room with all this playful energy. Full of charisma, he was wearing jeans and black leather jacket. Even though he was new to me, a few young adults in our group greeted him and seemed happy to see him there.

While I tried to play it cool, I was pretty intrigued by this interesting stranger.

At the time, I was dating a guy named Mark, an insurance salesman, whom I'd met at church. Tall and handsome, we'd hit it off immediately. Not long after, we were engaged. While it was fun at first, the relationship had grown increasingly toxic. His posture toward my singing ministry was, "Once she gets this singing thing out of her system, she can just be happy being my wife." He wasn't a bad guy, but I knew what I was called to do and didn't feel his support.

I was ready to walk.

It had been a few years since I'd won Voice of the 90s, and my career was growing. I was traveling, I had two CDs out that I was selling at concerts, and I was finally making money. I was also plugged in at church, where I'd serve on the singles worship team as often as I could. I had no plans to get singing out of my system.

In the middle of December Tim Clements, one of the pastors at church, caught me on the way out of church.

"Lisa," he said, "I've been hoping to catch up with you. Would you be able to sing for us on Christmas Eve?"

The invitation absolutely delighted me. I loved performing for audiences on the road, but being able to lead my own church family in worship always felt like a special blessing. I was thrilled to serve in that way, and immediately imagined the kind of vibe I wanted to create for worshipers that holy evening. I'd put together a three-piece group to sing a couple of mellow songs, including one entitled "The Star," recorded by my friend Kathy Mattea. Although the sanctuary at Capital Christian was a massive space, I wanted to create an atmosphere that felt really intimate. The moment he asked me, I could picture it in my mind.

"Tim," I responded with joy, "I would love to do that."

"I'm so glad!" he said. "What do you need from me?"

"Well," I mused, "I'd like to put together a three-piece band to sing a few songs. I'm not imagining *big*, I'm thinking of something more intimate."

Nodding, Tim agreed, "That sounds perfect. How about Deke, who plays the guitar? You know him?"

It was the guy with the black hair and black jacket. I'd asked a few friends about him since spotting him that night—and it turned out he was a musician.

"Yeah," I replied coolly, "I know who he is. I'll talk to him."

I tried to sound very nonchalant, all business, but inside I was excited to have the opportunity to meet him. I had noticed where he'd been sitting that morning, so I was able to catch up with him in the church lobby.

"Hey, can I have a second?" I asked, as he headed toward the door.

Turning my way, he flashed a smile. Sparks flew between us.

"Sure," he said. "What's up?"

"Well, I'm Lisa . . ." I began, flashing a smile of my own.

"I'm Deke," he replied. "Nice to meet you."

"Great to meet you," I said. "Pastor Tim invited me to sing on Christmas Eve, and I'd love it if you could play. What do you think?"

Pausing to think, he answered, "Bummer! I'll be out of town, visiting my mom in Vegas. Any other time I would have loved to have done it."

Feeling the chemistry between us, I promised, "I'll hold you to that. Let's try again sometime."

"Deal!" he agreed.

As I watched him leave, I had a pretty good feeling that we *were* going to play together one day.

The next time I saw Deke was the Sunday after Christmas, in the sanctuary.

"Hey," I said, "how was your Christmas?"

"It was good, thanks," he answered, adding, "and how was Christmas Eve?"

"Well," I answered humbly, "you should probably ask someone else."

I kind of hoped he would, because it had gone really well.

I added, "I got a few guys to play and I think it turned out really well."

Deke answered, "I'm sorry I missed it." Then, he added, "Hey, I'd love to hear more about your music. Would you want to grab coffee sometime?"

"Sure, that sounds great," I said.

The next Friday night, Deke and I went out. Before each of us had been saved, we'd been in some relationships that had gone too far sexually, and this time we wanted to do it right. So we invited a friend of Deke's, a girl named Judy, to go out with us. To keep it casual. To keep it pure. We all sat and chatted at a funky little coffee shop close to the church. I learned that Deke was in a metal band called Jesus Freaks, and that they had a song called "Hypocrite" that had reached Number 3 on the Christian rock charts. I'd be lying if I didn't say that was a little bit of a turn-on. And I was digging the whole country meets metal vibe we were sharing!

But beyond the cool rocker thing, I sensed such a love for the Lord in Deke's eyes. When I saw his transparent raw love for Christ, I was drawn to it. I tasted his passion and wanted to share it.

When they weren't performing, he and his band would attend secular metal concerts, where they'd hand out tracts to people before the concert. After the shows, they'd witness to people in the parking lot, inviting them to join them for coffee at a nearby joint. Or they'd go to bars around the time of last call, and spend time with anyone who was still there. Or, sometimes, they'd go to a Denny's restaurant at 2 a.m., lay a tract on every table—empty or full—and invite folks to join them in a big booth. The heart for others I saw in Deke was absolutely endearing. He lived alone in the upstairs part of a five-bedroom Victorian house downtown, and would even invite folks off the street who had no place to go to stay.

I loved who Deke was, and he loved who I was. I was especially grateful for his effusive support of my music ministry. When we were with my friends, at church, or out in public, I'd feel all warm and fuzzy when I'd overhear him bragging about me to others. Deke saw what was best in me, and reflected those qualities back to me. So when I was with him, I felt like my best self.

Deke and I quickly started spending more time together. Because he'd wrecked his truck, I'd pick him up for singles group or to grab a burger. It was easy to be together because the time we spent was fun and lighthearted. It wasn't long before I began to picture us sharing a life together. Being with someone who I could minister with was a dream I hadn't even dared to dream. At the time, it felt a little too good to be true.

While we were dating, I was flying back and forth to Nashville, getting ready to cut a third CD. On a layover in Dallas, I recognized recording producer Bill Traylor waiting at my gate. He'd produced several Southern gospel artists and had a Christian country label called Cheyenne Records under the parent record company, Homeland. I wasn't going to let the opportunity slip away.

Approaching him cautiously, I asked, "Are you Bill Traylor?"

Kindly, he confirmed he was. After introducing myself and chatting for a bit, I handed him my *Angels in Your Eyes* CD. Knowing he must be approached all the time by hopefuls like me, I prayed he'd give it a listen.

Thankfully, he did!

Back in Nashville, Bill went straight to Cheyenne's Artist and Representation office and set the CD down on the desk of Todd Payne.

"I just met this girl at the airport—" he began.

Picking up the CD, glancing at the cover, Todd confirmed, "Yeah, Lisa Daggs. I know her."

We'd connected years earlier, when I was performing and hustling there.

The next day, Todd contacted me to discuss possibilities.

Because Deke and I had begun to talk about sharing a life together, I couldn't wait to spill the juicy story the next time I saw him. As I gushed about what might come of the chance meeting, though, he clearly was not as enthused as I was. He didn't want to move to Nashville. I was disappointed we weren't on the same page, but I could no longer imagine a scenario in which I wasn't living and working in Music City. Sensing my determination, Deke began to realize that if he wanted to marry me, we'd be moving to Nashville.

But there were other little warning signs in the ways we related to one another that we both chose to ignore.

One night when we had dinner plans to go out with my best friend and her husband, Deke was late to pick me up. I was dressed up for an evening out on the town when he finally arrived. Having come straight from his job working for a tile contractor, I noticed a little salsa on his cheek, signaling that he'd just eaten at Taco Bell. He was also covered from head to toe in construction dust.

In a single second, I blew up at him, furious at his thoughtlessness. I wish I could say that kind of eruption was out of character for me. But in my early sobriety, unable to drink or use to manage my feelings, I would rage at times about situations over which I had no control. I cooled down but was still stressed about being late.

After he showered and changed, we pressed on and met my friends. But Deke iced me out at dinner, speaking to them but never once addressing me. Though not one word was spoken between us on the drive home, the following day I got a repentant message on my answering machine, "Baby, I'm so sorry, baby. That was uncalled for. I won't ever do it again." After listening to the apologies ramble on, I saved the message. I had a strange feeling that I'd need to hear it again. And again.

Though neither one of us wanted to see it, the toxic pattern was part of our dance. He'd do some stupid, thoughtless thing. My reaction would be out of proportion at times, but the punishment he dished out far outsized my crime. He'd beg for forgiveness. At some point after we'd made up, we'd inevitably run through the whole cycle again. We loved each other, but neither of us was coming to the table with a full set of emotional skills to work through conflict in a healthy way.

One person who knew us both had the courage to express concern about our relationship. Pam, a friend of mine from our singles group at church, asked me to meet her for lunch one day at The Good Earth. After we'd ordered and sat down, she began to share her concern with me Though she didn't know Deke well, Pam had noticed a few things in him and seen a few interactions between us that concerned her. I don't think anyone in their right mind ever seeks out these kinds of conversations, but because Pam was devoted to the Lord—like my mom—she was faithful to respond to the prompting the Holy Spirit had laid on her heart. Over soup and salad, she cautioned me about marrying Deke. She was worried that he wasn't who I thought he was. Of course, the whole conversation was awkward and uncomfortable for both of us. Though I had no interest in what felt like her unfounded judgments, I nodded politely as I sipped my soup. When we finally parted ways in the parking lot, I thanked her for her concern.

And then I simply dismissed her warning.

One Saturday night about four months into dating, Deke picked me up and surprised me by telling me he was taking me out to dinner in San Francisco. We cruised along, singing our lungs out to Keith Green's "You Put This Love in My Heart" as we drove through the streets of San Francisco, and I realized we were getting closer to my favorite restaurant, Sabellas, on the wharf. In a rare fancy moment, Deke even let the valet park his truck!

We started out by ordering clam chowder, one of my favorite items. When we started talking about our relationship, I had an inkling what might be coming. Sensing that he might propose, I wanted to make sure there were no secrets between us. Though I'd shared some of my past, I wanted to make sure he'd seen the whole messy picture, so he would know what he might be getting into. After I unloaded the worst of it, I waited to see if he'd freak out. If he'd bail. If he'd run.

He didn't.

Between dinner and dessert, Deke dropped to his knee and pulled out a small leather box.

He began by telling me how much he loved me. Then, holding the box in front of him, opening it to show me a ring, he asked, "Lisa, will you marry me?"

"Yes. Yes. Yes!"

Three yeses.

Rising to his feet, he looked like the happiest man alive.

Sitting back down, Deke pulled the ring out of the box. While the diamond was beautiful, the rest—which actually looked like a clunky *man*-ring—left a bit to be desired. (I am a girly-girl.) Deke told me the story behind it—and it actually *was* a clunky man-ring! My dad had won it, probably in a card game, and the gorgeous diamond was still in its original setting. My dad sold it to Deke, giving him more than a fair price for the gorgeous stone, when he'd driven to Concord to ask permission to marry me. (After he received my three yeses, he had it reset into a Lisa-sized ring.)

Eight months after we met, Deke and I had a beautiful wedding in the gorgeous sanctuary at Capital Christian Center. It was November 11, 1996, the sixth anniversary of my sobriety. In fact, staying clean and sober was one of the promises I made to Deke at our wedding. We were thrilled to jump into the life of love and ministry we were certain God had planned for us and began our married life moving to Nashville, sharing an apartment with my friend Julia as we looked for a home of our own .

Having dated guys who drank too much, guys who used to much, guys who'd belittled me, and ones who weren't believers, I felt like I'd won the lottery when I married Deke. And the fact that we shared a love for God and passion for expressing it through music felt like delicious icing on the creamy white wedding cake. Deke was someone who "got" who I was and what I'd been called to do. He encouraged me to pursue the dream God had knit into my heart. He played alongside me at various gigs when he could. He made sure I had all the right electronic equipment. He never stopped raving to others about the ways God had gifted me and was using me. It was clear to me that God had given me Deke to empower me to do what God had designed me to do. He also made a promise before we married that he didn't need alcohol and he would never drink again.

Is there someone in your life who inspires, encourages, and equips you to use your gifts for the kingdom? It doesn't have to be a spouse. Maybe when you were young you had a parent who noticed your gift with words, or with crayons, or with problem solving. Or maybe you had a friend who recognized gifts in you that you hadn't yet recognized in yourself. Or perhaps you've had a mentor who fanned the flame God ignited within you, encouraging you to shine for His glory. God is faithful to provide people in our lives who will help us do what we were born to do. For some that might be building and owning a small business. For others, it might be raising children to know and love God. Some people will discover their passions and callings as they offer their gifts in service of others. And some will glorify God in the workplace: filing and phoning, cooking and creating, drawing and designing, selling and speaking. God equips each one of us with all we need to live out our purpose, and that includes providing people who inspire, encourage, and equip us as we use our gifts for the sake of the ones God loves.

My mother has always been a person like that. She had a vision for who God made me to be, even when I was rebelling and going my own way. From my earliest years, I never doubted that my mom saw me, knew me, and loved me.

I'd not had that experience with my dad, and my heart had always ached for his attention. His approval. His love. He knew I sang, but he'd never seemed particularly interested in or supportive of what I was trying to build and achieve. Sadly, the season of our relationship when we interacted the most frequently was when he was selling me drugs while I lived in Nashville. Even though I was now a married adult woman, on the inside I still yearned for his attention and affection. Having been unable to extract it from him for decades, I'd given up on the possibility of a meaningful relationship with my dad.

I didn't know if it was possible, but part of me dared to dream that it was.

Chapter 16

THE GAITHERS

On the six-hour drive from my home in Smyrna, Tennessee, to Alexandria, Indiana, I was bubbling with anticipation. Another door had opened for me, and I was ready to bolt through it in my fringe-trimmed beige leather boots!

The man who'd held this door ajar for me was Bill Traylor, who I'd met a year earlier at the Dallas airport before being signed to Cheyenne Records. Because I knew Bill, I was able to benefit from his rich relational networks, especially the one he had with Bill and Gloria Gaither.

At the time, they were working on a special project called *Bill & Gloria and the Homecoming Friends.* The vision was to bring together a host of gospel and southern gospel artists, including Andrae' Crouch, Shirley Caesar, The Gatlins, The Oakridge Boys, Randy Travis, Babbie Mason, Ronnie Milsap, and Michael English—a beautiful, star-studded lineup of industry giants. I'd admired many of them for years.

So when they invited me to join one of the videos they were filming at the Gaithers' home studio in Alexandria, I jumped at the chance.

As I drove, I fantasized about what the weekend held. We'd be recording for three days, and I'd be rubbing shoulders with the legendary Gaither family. I'd met Gloria briefly, several years earlier when I attended a conference at Oral Roberts University, but never in a million years could I have imagined I'd be singing *with* them at their hometown studio.

I arrived just after lunch on Friday. As I looked around the room, I saw legends like The Cathedrals, J.D. Sumner, The Happy Goodmans, Hovie Lister, The McDuff Brothers, Dottie Rambo, Jake Hess, and Bob Cain. When the producer gathered us up to give us instructions, he emphasized how important it was that our appearance remain consistent over the three-day shoot. For a girl who likes to get her fashion on, it was a sacrifice I was willing to make. Thankfully, I felt great in the outfit I'd chosen: a buttoned-up long-sleeve cream shirt, a tightly knit crocheted vest with silk ties, a crinkly cream-colored skirt to my ankles, and those fringed beige boots. Cognizant of the classy company, I was careful not to show any cleavage or armpits. Or even legs. I wanted all the bases to be covered, so to speak!

A piano was positioned on the main floor of the studio, and behind it was a semi-circle of seats lifted up on carpeted risers for greater visibility. Each of the performers was assigned a chair we'd occupy for the three days, making it easier for editing, so the shots would show us as the "audience" for whoever was performing.

The opportunity of being the new girl on the docket was equally scary and thrilling. I'd suggested to Bill Traylor that I might sing "Hands on the Plow," a country song that really rocks, and he thought it was great. On Saturday, I felt my heart racing when I stepped onto the main stage to sing. I move a lot when I sing, and I didn't want to offend anyone. I had to remind myself to keep my feet on the ground so I'd stay in the camera frame.

When I heard the opening bars of the song, my head started moving and my toes started tapping. Although I was committed to being myself, I was of course also anxious about what the others would think. As I got into my groove, I saw a few eyebrows raise, as if to say, *Well, this is different.* They weren't wrong.

I noticed Walt Mills from Trinity Broadcast Network smiling in support. That was encouraging. Within moments, any anxiety I'd brought with me had melted away as I got to do what I was born to do. Halfway through the song, everyone on the risers was clapping along. As I belted out the final bars, I got a sincere wink of approval from George Younce, the well-loved bass singer of the Cathedrals. At the time I interpreted the gesture to mean, "Well done." Had we been recording today, I think he might have said, "Get it, girl!" The applause from the group as I handed the mic back to Mr. Gaither and returned to my seat was like balm for my heart. This was the precious moment of affirmation I'd been waiting so long to receive.

After my performance we broke for lunch. As I was filling my plate in the buffet line, Bill Gaither's right-hand man, Ben Spear, sidled up next to me and whispered in my ear, "You hit a home run, girl!" I felt like I had, but of course it was great to hear it from someone of his stature!

After we wrapped the next day, Bill Gaither took me aside, hugged my neck, and confirmed, "I love your spirit."

That was the beginning of a beautiful friendship with Bill and Gloria. They invited me to go on tour with them several times over the next ten years. We traveled all over the United States, the Caribbean, even South Africa, and shot at least twenty-five videos. Though I often sang as part of the group, I was invited to perform solos on half a dozen videos, as well as in the Live Homecoming Concerts.

One of the hard-earned lessons I share with all new performers now, I learned the first time I ever sang on stage with the group of friends! I'd sung during the first half of the concert at Arco Arena in my hometown of Sacramento, and the audience ate it up. (And I was seven-and-a-half months pregnant at the time!) During the next number, Bill leaned over and whispered in my ear, "You got another song?" The words that should have been music to my ears fell like an axe! Though there were hundreds of songs in my heart and on my lips, I hadn't brought the music tracks for more than the specific assignment I'd been given. Wanting to please, longing to perform, I was crushed. So now I always coach new performers, "Always bring more than one track!"

The investment the Gaithers made in me wasn't out of character for them: they were known throughout the industry for generously helping artists launch careers. What I gained from them is incalculable. Gloria was filled with so much wisdom and kindness that whenever she spoke, I'd lean in to hear what she had to say.

Back home in Smyrna, Deke and I were preparing for an exciting addition to our family. We were eager to welcome a child into our home and into our hearts.

As I began to dream about spending time at home with a baby, I was offered a local opportunity that felt like a gift from God. Herman Bailey was an entertainer who co-hosted a popular show in Palm Beach, *The Herman and Sharon Show*. Herman also managed TV39 in Nashville, and invited me to consider hosting a thirty-minute show called *Lisa Daggs Backstage*, on which I'd interview musicians and wrap with an invitation to know Christ. I was thrilled to accept.

The set was decorated to appear like just about every "backstage" looks everywhere: microphone, lights, a ladder, and other paraphernalia that ends up behind the curtain. Some of my guests were from the Grand Ole Opry, like Lulu Roman and Skeeter Davis. I also welcomed mainstream performers like Paul Overstreet, James Bonamy, and The Hinsons, and talked with contemporary Christian artists, like Newsboys and Big Tent Revival. We'd sit on comfy overstuffed chairs and chat as if we were in my living room. We'd explore their lives, how they got started in the business, and their biggest successes before issuing an altar call.

While a lot of people told me how much they liked the show, especially dishing about the business, I always wondered if the outreach at the end was making a difference in the lives of viewers. That was more true than ever when the show was cancelled, because there weren't enough people calling in. However, reruns ran for a year and a half!

One Sunday I was really dragging. Deke and I were on the tail end of a ten-week tour and scheduled to do a concert that night at our own church. I'd had strep throat for over a week, but I'd continued to sing at concerts, saving my voice during the day and then using everything I had at the shows. When we arrived for the sound check at 4 p.m., I noticed a man walk in at the back of the church. Clean-shaven, wearing a sport coat and slacks, he walked down the center aisle of the sanctuary carrying a huge Bible—beaming.

"Hi, Miss Lisa," he said.

I wasn't feeling well and wished I could make a speedy exit, Still, I put on a smile and greeted him.

He continued, "I want to let you know that no matter how tired you are, you're still making a difference and it's worth it."

Okay, even though I didn't know where he was going with that comment, he had my attention.

"Thank you," I replied, "that is so kind of you to say."

He went on to share his story. "I was blind drunk one night when I was watching your TV show a few years ago. I don't know exactly what you said, but when you spoke it went right into my heart and I knew I needed to get help."

"Wow!" I interjected.

He kept sharing, "I checked into the Nashville Rescue Mission. Been clean and sober a year."

I was blown away by God's goodness. Not only that, but he hadn't even seen one of our live shows: his life had been transformed by one of the *reruns*! I was reminded that no amount of hustle, drive, or hard work could ever touch the power of God's Spirit in people's lives. While one part of me knew that already, I needed to see it up close and personal that day, and hear it with my own ears so I would continue to depend on it to minister through me.

The next day God gave me the words for "Even When You're Not Here"—a song about someone who's fallen far from grace, and yet is touched by a guiding hand that reaches through time to find and guide him.

We don't always see the fruit of our obedience in the moments that we are living out our callings.

Maybe you've poured your energies into an outreach ministry to college students, but aren't seeing anyone come to Christ. Or perhaps you tutor a child after school whose chaotic household makes it difficult for him to succeed. Maybe someone you led to the Lord returns to a life of sin. Or it could be that you use your writing, speaking, instrument, or testimony to minister to audiences, like me, and you aren't seeing any fruit from the seeds you've planted.

Beloved, *keep on in obedience*. You may not ever see easily quantifiable "results." But God's economy is different than ours. Your job is not to evaluate the fruit; it is only to be faithful. You do your part, and let God worry about the fruit-bearing.

Trusting God to provide of fruit was a lesson He would continue to teach me.

Chapter 17

TRUSTING GOD FOR FAITH

Deke and I had been married less than a year when we bought our first home together in Smyrna. Situated in a cute little neighborhood, it was a three-bedroom, two-bath home with a bonus room over a garage that we used as a music room. When we moved in the sparse furnishings from our apartment, there was a lot of extra space in every room. Gradually, we would add furniture—but we were most eager to add a nursery for the baby we were hoping and praying for.

We were living in our new home when we first conceived. We were elated! On my first prenatal visit, the doctor checked my progesterone levels. They registered at nineteen.

"And . . . ?" I queried, having no idea if we were aiming for one hundred or twenty.

"That's okay," he said. "Nineteen is okay."

It wasn't the rave review I'd hoped for, but I'd take it.

A few weeks later, Deke and I arrived home from a concert late Friday night and fell into bed. The clock glowed 5:13 a.m. when I awoke to horrible cramping pain in my abdomen. Without waking my husband, I stumbled to the bathroom. When I pulled down my underwear, I saw red stains.

"Deke!" I called as I sat down on the toilet.

Hearing the desperation in my voice surprised me.

I felt something pass into the toilet. Peeking down, I saw red clots falling out of my body and into the water below.

"Deke!" I screamed, louder this time.

Deke jumped out of bed and rushed to my side.

"I'm bleeding!" I'd begun to sob.

Dropping down, Deke placed both his hands on my knees.

"It's okay, baby, it's okay. We'll be okay."

Though no words could fix what was going wrong, I felt like we were together, as one, in the horror we were facing.

"Babe," he cooed, "I'm so sorry."

His face told me he was as crushed as I was. He reached up to touch my face. As I wept, he straightened and gently rubbed my back.

"It's gonna be okay . . ." he said soothingly.

Although I was in too much emotional agony to process his kindness until much later, he was the greatest pillar of strength and compassion I could have hoped for in those moments.

When we got to the hospital, an hour later, the news I'd dreaded was confirmed: I had miscarried. Our pastor and his wife came to be with us at the hospital. Crushed by sorrow and forced to wait six months before attempting another pregnancy, I grieved.

Two days later I was scheduled to sing "How Great Thou Art" in worship. While our pastor certainly gave me an out, suggesting he could find someone else to sing, I insisted. There was something holy about singing those lyrics. Tears dripped off my chin as I sang, holding the precious one I wouldn't get to meet on this earth in my heart. About a dozen people in the sanctuary knew why the performance was particularly poignant for me. The moment I stepped offstage, Deke embraced me.

As soon as we were allowed to try to conceive again, we did. We'd spent the interim reading every book we could get our hands on about increasing the likelihood of conception and praying for twins. Because my mom is a twin, we knew it was a real possibility for us.

Several months later, the thin pink line on another home pregnancy test confirmed that I was again with child. At my first ultrasound, Deke held my hand as the radiologist interpreted the nondescript gray blobs on the screen.

"Look at that," she said, putting her gloved finger on the monitor. "Two yolk sacks!"

"Wait, what?" I asked.

"You're having twins!" she announced.

God's goodness overwhelmed me: He was restoring what the locusts had eaten.

About six weeks later, we flew to Las Vegas to share Christmas with Deke's mother and mine. We all worshipped together on Christmas Eve, and the story of God entering the world through a pregnant woman had never been more poignant to me. God's ways were truly mind-bending.

The next morning, I was relaxing with Deke in the living room when I had to take a potty break. That's when I noticed bright red spotting in my underpants.

"Deke," I called out to him, "will you come here?"

He read my face before I showed him the evidence. We'd wanted desperately to believe that the loss of our first child had been random and unpreventable, but this scary sign suggested there might be more to it. Because the spotting started lightly, we didn't know immediately if I was losing our twins. Our doctor suggested see him when we got home the next day. By the time we got there, the twins were gone.

This loss felt different. I have to chalk that up to God's steadfast presence with us. It was also a comfort to have my mom nearby. It wasn't quite as traumatic as our first miscarriage; it was a time of shared, gentle stillness and sadness. I remember praying, "If this gives me more empathy for other women who have experienced this same great loss, then not my will but Yours."

But Christmas morning, Lord?

The irony felt cruel.

A week later, I scheduled an appointment with a high-risk obstetrician at Vanderbilt named Dr. Cornelia Graves.

"I'm so glad you came to see me," she said, welcoming us to sit across from the mahogany desk in her office. "You obviously don't have a problem getting pregnant, so it seems like there could be a problem with your progesterone level."

A little bell went off in my head.

"But," I protested, "my doctor said nineteen was 'okay.' I remember he said it was okay."

If only repeating the information had been able to change the outcome.

"No," she said carefully, "I want to see it up closer to forty. Especially in those first weeks when the baby nestles into the uterine wall and gets attached."

Deke and I exchanged glances.

"I want you to give your body six months to heal before trying again. Then, call me as soon as you get pregnant."

Pregnant.

The word that used to be filled with such hope and possibility hung in the air between us.

Could I even face being pregnant again?

As we left Dr. Graves's office that day, I had no other choice than to give that possibility back to God, not knowing if I could face another possible miscarriage.

My precious friend Karen Mitchell had lost a daughter, Samantha, at the tender age of one year. Before I'd ever conceived myself, I'd sung at her funeral. Samantha had been Karen's second baby. During that season our losses, though different, knit us together. Karen was one of my biggest cheerleaders on the excruciating fertility journey.

The month my period was finally a week late, I called her.

"It's only been about seven days late," I confessed, "but of course every day I get a little more hopeful. But do I even *want* to be hopeful?"

"Go to Walmart, girl!" she said. "Get that pregnancy test! Then call me!"

If a trip to Walmart can be a holy pilgrimage, this one was.

Two hours later I was looking at a white stick that had tested positive for pregnancy.

My first call was to Deke at work, knowing he'd probably be breaking for lunch. Our elation was cautious, but genuine. Before we hung up, we prayed for God's protection over our child.

Karen was next, of course, and she screamed when I gave her the news.

Then I called my mom.

And that was enough. It had been brutal to tell all the friends who'd known of each of our pregnancies that we'd lost our babies; I wanted to hold this one closer to the vest. There would be plenty of time to celebrate with our community when our little one was born.

Every Friday I visited Dr. Graves.

Every Friday my blood was drawn.

And every Friday she'd prescribe a specific dosage of the progesterone suppository that would keep my levels strong.

I continued to get bigger and bigger; Deke's love and affection for me during our third pregnancy matched his tender care during our miscarriages. When my belly swelled, we'd make a huge donut of pillows on the bed so I could lie face-down with my belly in the middle, and he would rub my back and my feet. I loved being married and I loved being pregnant.

Both Deke and I wanted our mothers to be with us in Tennessee for the birth.. But babies really don't care about either grandmothers' schedules or airline fares. And while I knew that some women who want to control the timing of their babies' births choose to artificially induce labor, I really wanted mine to progress naturally. And that meant my water would break when our baby was ready to arrive.

At my last scheduled appointment with Dr. Graves before my due date, I told her our moms were flying in, but that I didn't want to induce. I thought I saw a little flash of an idea erupt on her face.

"I'll tell you what to do," she said. "The night before they come, I want you to make your husband very happy—if you know what I mean!"

"Okay," I said, taking mental notes.

"And after that," she continued, "I want you to walk for a long time! I mean really walk for miles."

I asked, "And how does that help?"

"You'll lose your mucus plug," she explained, "and go into labor naturally."

So on the night of my mom's arrival, we'll just say I followed doctor's orders. And she was right! Then we drove to the airport and I walked to the very last gate in the terminal, where my mom's flight was scheduled to arrive. When she walked off the plane, I flashed her a big smile and lifted up my shirt to flash her my forty-weeks pregnant belly.

If memory serves, the very first words she said to me, as she giggled, were, "Put your shirt down!"

After we got home, my early labor continued, feeling like little "bites" around my middle throughout the night. The contractions that began at long, irregular intervals eventually became regular enough for us to throw my packed bag in the car and go to the hospital. And by "us," of course, I mean Deke, me, and our moms!

As I was standing at the admissions desk, I felt warm liquid trickling down my leg.

"Oh my gosh!" I exclaimed. "My water broke!"

The receptionist in front of me, not seeing a puddle of water on the floor, said, "I don't think so."

Although it had been a few years since I'd peed in my pants, I knew I would have been able to *stop it* if that's what had been happening. And there was no stopping that warm waterfall.

Well, that little stunt got me admitted to a labor room!

We were there a long time. When I was dilated to almost eight centimeters, my labor stopped progressing. The doctor needed to see ten before allowing me to push. It was already pretty painful, and fifteen hours in to the labor I hadn't yet taken anything for pain. I wanted to give birth naturally, but when Dr. Graves suggested an epidural, I was relieved.

After twenty-two hours, when I was finally authorized to push, my small hips made delivery difficult. So Dr. Graves decided to use forceps—basically huge salad tongs—to help pull our baby into the world. As our little one began to crown, Deke gave me a play-by-play report.

"Lisa!" he shouted, "I can see a full head of black hair!"

When our baby finally entered the world with a final push from me, the doctor caught her and announced, "It's a girl!"

Tears of joy streamed down all our cheeks, following the same tracks as the ones we'd shed over the loss of our baby's three siblings.

As Dr. Graves was busy sewing up my insides, two nurses carried our daughter over to the exam table to inspect her. They were soon joined by several pediatricians who'd rushed in, which concerned me.

"Deke," I asked, "what's going on?"

I heard one of the pediatricians saying, coolly, "We're not impressed yet."

Deke stepped closer to listen in, and learned that the "problem" was she hadn't *cried* yet. While of no concern to overwhelmed moms with colicky babies, it was apparently a problem in the delivery room. They needed to hear a baby cry before they'd sign off.

"She's beautiful," Deke reported proudly, unfazed by our silent child. "She has these big dark eyes that are rolling around from side to side checking out everything in the room!"

One of the doctors pinched our girl on the heel. That did the trick! She cried and impressed everyone.

Once she was cleaned off, the nurse wrapped her in a standard hospital-issue receiving blanket and gently laid her down on my chest. Gazing into those gorgeous dark eyes, I decided she was simply perfect.

"So what's her name?!" Deke's mom asked.

We exchanged glances, and Deke nodded to signal that I could do the honors.

"Her name is Faith Ilene," I announced. My middle name is Ilene, which means "giver of light," and Faith really was a tribute to my mom, who was an absolute pillar of godly strength for me and so many others.

I was released from the hospital the next day as tornado warnings sounded over Nashville. When our Faith was just three days old, we all holed up in a closet listening to a transistor radio with me sitting on a donut pillow. It was the stuff of which every new mother dreams. Faith Ilene had taken our life by storm.

She quickly became the joy of my life. When Faith was three or four weeks old, I sang, "You are my sunshine, my only sunshine . . ."

She looked up at me, her little nose all wet from nursing.

". . . you make me happy, when skies are gray . . ."

Or have funnel clouds.

"You'll never know dear, how much I love you . . ." I sang, voice rising.

And at that pause in the melody, my little baby—who all the parenting books said was too young to give a smile that meant anything other than she'd passed gas—gave me the biggest grin. This mama's heart just melted.

But because I'm not that mom who blindly thinks my child is the greatest genius who ever lived, I tried again.

"You are my sunshine . . ."

And when I paused at exactly the same point in the song— "You'll never know, dear, how much I love you"—a huge grin spread across her face again. Imagine a little smile with her gums still latched onto me, cooing, "Eeeee!"

Okay, she *was* pretty special.

When I was single, I never imagined the twists and turns my path would take—that I'd go through rehab or be faced with the threat of prison. I couldn't have seen the unique opportunities to perform and record I would be offered. And I certainly would not have imagined suffering the heart-wrenching miscarriages that Deke and I weathered. I begged God for a child, and when I finally held that smiling savant, I knew exactly Who had delivered her into my arms.

Maybe your life has not unfolded as you imagined it would when you were younger. Actually, that's more likely a *probability* than a possibility! You may have imagined you'd be married by a certain age, and you weren't. Or maybe, like me, you desperately yearned for children, and your road to parenting has been bumpier than you expected. Maybe you hoped to do one thing professionally, but because of circumstances beyond your control you've had to explore other options. Or it could be that you are living without the one person you never would have imagined living without.

One thing the Lord has shown me on this journey is that He can be trusted with my dreams.

And He can be trusted with yours.

Whether it's a hope you've held since you were a child or a freshly budding possibility that is sprouting up in your heart today, you can release your clenched fists and give that dream to God. My experience has taught me that it's not a one-time process, either. You might have to do it every day. Maybe every hour. I do know that God's ways are not our ways, and His thoughts are not our thoughts. I'm also convinced that God's heart for you is kind.

So carve out space to get alone with Him and release what you've held so tightly into His care. Or start each day by lifting your hands to the Heavens and spreading them wide open—both to release what you've been gripping and also to receive whatever He has for you.

Faith brought light into our lives and being her mother was a delight to my heart. But other relationships in my life were about to bring such weighty blows that it was not clear whether they would survive.

Chapter 18

DAD GOES HOME

After Deke and I married, I continued to make time to visit my dad at the VA home in Yountville. He had a heart attack after his strokes, and I knew his health was fragile. Part of me knew he was dying and our days together were numbered. So right before Faith's first birthday we packed up and moved back to California to be closer to family in Sacramento

As unlikely as it sounds, in some ways that's when my dad became for me the kind of father I'd always wanted and needed. Maybe it was because I finally had access to him. I don't know. But more and more often, I found myself turning to him when I had a decision to make. Although he wasn't a "fixer," he always helped me think through my options.

"If you choose A, then most likely this will happen . . ."

"If you choose B, this is probably where it would go . . ."

"And then if you choose option C, the most likely outcome would be . . ."

He'd always wrap up these moments of guidance with the words, "But it's your decision, Punkin'."

And he wasn't just present for me when I showed up at the VA home. He began to take great pleasure and pride in following my journey. When Deke and I were out on the road, my dad would track our journey. I might pick up the phone after a trip and hear him ask, "So how was the concert in Dallas last night?" When his world became very small, really limited the four walls of his tight quarters, he found meaning and purpose in following me through his web-TV.

I also saw him reaching out to care for others. For a few years, he had a job checking vets' membership cards at the dining hall entrance and acting as cashier for the family members joining them for a meal. I noticed the way he cared for those who'd shuffle by with their heads hanging low.

"Hi, Bill."

"How's your day going, Tom?"

"How are you today, George?"

"Thanks, Larry, good to see you."

Eventually, one of these more reserved men would give my dad a little nod.

When he kept after them long enough, he might see a big break-through, like one of them asking, "Hi Bob, how are you doing?"

That. Was. Huge. He felt so good about having the opportunity to lift the spirits of other vets.

And when he was well enough, my dad was even able to come to a few of my local concerts!

The one outing with him etched in my memory forever was when he and my mom attended a concert I gave at New Life Church in Rancho Cordova. I loved stealing glimpses of his face while I was singing and sharing. He was such a proud papa. At the end of the evening, I invited those in the audience who didn't know Christ to join me in praying the sinners' prayer.

On the way home, he told me and Mom, "I did it."

"Did what?" we asked.

"I prayed that prayer at the end," he said proudly, almost like a small boy.

My dad had heard me extend that invitation at other concerts, but as far as I knew he'd never responded. Needless to say, we were thrilled. My heart was full. I was amazed by the way the Lord allowed me to be a part of that most special night.

My dad had Christ, and I had my dad. After years of longing for his attention, I didn't take his interest for granted. Although he couldn't fix the past, his care for me in that season meant the world to me and helped me heal.

Each November on his birthday, I'd perform a concert at the VA home called the Bob Daggs Birthday Bash. Sometimes we'd be in the infirmary. Other times it would be held in the Alzheimer's lock-down unit, and sometimes in the game room. Once it was in the chapel. The home's activities team posted posters a week ahead of time, which made my dad feel like the fat cat with the celebrity daughter. He even wore a T-shirt with my picture on it as he drove around in his electric scooter, carrying the flyers and being the promoter!

Unfortunately, my father's health continued to deteriorate, which was hard to watch. I remember visiting him at Queen of the Valley Hospital in Napa after his aorta was replaced. They had cut the temperature in the room down in order to lower his body, and when I visited it was hard not to imagine we were in the morgue. He was just so cold and pale.

I also began noticing his mental faculties slipping away.

After being diagnosed with prostate cancer, he was so weak that doctors predicted his heart would give out before the cancer got him. During that season he began receiving hospice care and was on more medications than I could count. During one of my last visits, I'd noticed that his skin was a grayish color.

One Thursday afternoon in 2003, my mom and I went for a visit with little Faith, by then a wiggly three-year-old. We drove up to see him waiting for us impatiently in front of the hospital in his wheelchair. We were about fifteen minutes late and he was upset. He'd lodged one of his wheels in the flower bed and couldn't get out without some help. I was happy to oblige and—with his half-cocked smirk and rolled eyes—he let me help him, somewhat humbly. It was kinda funny.

The nurse met us downstairs, too and pulling me aside, the whispered, "He's been waiting for you. He's saved up all of his energy for this short trip."

My dad's face lit up when he saw us, especially Faith. Though he was delighted we'd come to visit, I believe in the back of his mind he knew he was on borrowed time.

"Do you feel like lunch at the Soda Shoppe?" I asked in a perky voice, as if hoping to recharge his battery with some of my extra energy.

Despite his exhaustion, Dad started zipping down the cement pathway toward the Soda Shoppe. We struggled to keep up with him, jogging in our heels! I keep a picture of that day of my dad, mom and Faith, and me. There are two chocolate malts between us, and all four of us are sucking on straws jammed into one of the two glasses.

When we finally helped dad back into bed and said goodbye, I breathed a prayer of thanks to God for the sacred time we'd shared together.

Later that week, Deke, Faith, and I were at home watching the Oakland Raiders play the Tampa Bay Buccaneers in the Super Bowl, waiting for the halftime commercials, when a very intimate knowing began to swell in my heart.

I looked at Faith playing with toys on the floor and told Deke, "I have to go see my dad. He's dying."

Like my mom's "knowings" before mine, I was touched with a supernatural awareness that my dad's time on this earth was drawing to a close.

A bit startled, Deke agreed, "Okay. I've got Faith. Do what you have to do."

When I slipped into my dad's room, he looked very thin. I noticed two sticky wooden sticks, showing traces of the grape morphine popsicle he'd been offered to help ease his pain. The nurse stepped out into the hallway when I arrived. Quietly pulling a chair closer to his bed, I watched him for about an hour before he opened his eyes and saw me.

Smiling, he leaned over and said, "Hi Punkin'."

Heart warmed, I grinned and said, "Hi, dad."

After a few minutes of filling him on what Faith was up to, the hospice nurse silently motioned for me to join her in the hallway.

"He's really struggling to hang on," she said.

Surprised he could have failed so much in just three days, I reported, "On Thursday he was such a bullet! Today is *so* different."

Nodding, she explained, "He saved all of his energy for that outing. Knowing it was the last."

Had it been too much? Should we not have come? But I knew that there was nothing my dad would rather do than sip chocolate malts with Faith and me—not to mention Mom. While it sounds a little strange to say that, considering how long they'd been divorced, after he'd left our family my dad realized he'd walked away from the best woman ever. In those final years, if we were out in public and he saw someone he knew, he'd always introduce my mom with pride, saying, "This is the mother of my children." Despite all that had happened between them, they were still each other's first loves.

Returning to sit with him, I noticed a bowl of oranges on the rolling tray beside his bed.

"Can I help you with these?" I asked.

"Sure," he said. "That would be nice."

Pulling the peel back off of each slice, I held the succulent pieces up to his mouth so he could receive them. Unfortunately, whatever went into his mouth went right through him. So after he finished the orange, I helped the nurse change him. After he was clean and dry, I climbed into the empty bed beside him and scooched over to be closer to him. We ended up talking until I saw his eyelids drooping. I walked over to his bed, gave him a kiss on the forehead, let him know I'd be sleeping nearby, and left the room so he could rest for the night.

The VA home offered rooms to guests for just twenty-five dollars a night, and it was a relief to be able to stay so near to him.

When I got to his room the next morning, the hospice nurse was blotting his forehead with a damp cloth. She set it down on his bedside table to make room for me to visit.

Feeling like the little girl who wanted nothing more than to be close to her daddy, I quietly asked the nurse, "Can I crawl in there with him?"

"Of course," she agreed, and left the room to give us some space.

Slipping off my sandals, I crawled up into the bed beside my dad. When I cuddled in as close as I could get to him and hugged his belly, he put his left arm around me and patted my back. Cheek-to-cheek, I whispered into his ear, "I love you, Dad."

"I love you, too, Punkin'," he assured me.

"Daddy," I cooed, "it's okay. If you're tired, and you want to let go, you can. I promise I'll take care of Mom for you."

When my dad fell asleep, I prayed a prayer releasing him into the loving arms of Jesus, and quietly climbed out of bed to head home. There were as many tears spilling out of me on the way home as there had been on the way to see him.

In the most absurd timing, Deke and I had plans to go to Hawaii the following day. Our friend was watching Faith so we could get a long-awaited vacation. I considered canceling the trip, but our marriage was in a difficult place and we needed the opportunity to reconnect. As my relationship with my father was being healed and growing, my marriage to Deke had been deteriorating.

Our flight left San Francisco at eight o'clock Tuesday morning. As we lifted up over the ocean, I had a strong sense that I wasn't going to see my dad alive again.

We arrived at our hotel on Oahu an hour before sunset, and I was itchy to get to the beach to watch the sun go down. I adore sunsets and the way their beauty marks the end of the gift of another day. This sunset, in particular, was important to me.

"Come on, come on," I pressed, "walk with me. Let's go to the beach. Come on, baby."

Despite my pleas, Deke slowed his stride and ended walking a half a block behind me, as if we weren't together.

"Come on," I continued to plead, "we're gonna miss it."

We finally cleared the line of palm trees and made it to the beach. As the sun began to drop down toward the horizon, Deke walked away to sit on a rock about fifty yards from where I was sitting in the sand. Feeling confused by his distance, I walked over to join him. Just as the glowing pink orb dipped out of sight, I said, "My dad's dying."

The following morning I got a call in our hotel room from my mom. As I picked up the phone, I knew it wasn't going to be good news.

"Lisa," she said, with a catch in her voice, "I'm so sorry."

I started to weep quietly.

"Yesterday," she explained, "Larry, Faith and I visited Dad, but he wasn't speaking. Lisa, you were the last person in our family to talk to him."

Although I was grateful for those moments, I envied my brother Larry for being there at the end.

Because we wouldn't hold a memorial service for several more weeks, I decided to finish the vacation I'd worked so hard to plan. I'd arranged the rental car, a day cruise, dinner reservations, trips, and a luau on our last night on the island. But Deke remained as disengaged as he'd been on our first day. Not only did I feel like I was weathering the loss of my father alone, but I was essentially vacationing alone.

The day we left, we were using adjacent restrooms before the shuttle arrived to take us back to the airport. Because the rooms echoed loudly, I heard Deke talking on the phone to our bass player, who also was weathering a difficult season in his marriage.

That's when I heard Deke complain, "Dude, you think you've got it bad?! I'm in paradise with this bitch!"

What?!

Did he really just say that?

Who is this guy I'm married to?

All of a sudden I had a flashback to a day in 2001. Faith was sixteen months old, and I was still nursing. It was late and I was tired, so I headed to bed. A few minutes later, Deke started practicing his guitar in the kitchen—with an amp. The third time I came out and asked him to please turn it down, he picked me up by the neck and walked me down the hall to the back bedroom. My feet were completely off of the ground all the way down the hallway. As he tossed me in the room, he said "Don't you dare come out of here again! "

This wasn't the man who'd supported me through the losses of our babies and rejoiced with me when Faith was born.

Whoever was talking on the phone in the bathroom was a stranger.

I was devastated by the ugly words that swirled through my mind, haunting me on the whole trip home. I don't recall speaking one word to him on the flight back.

Before we landed in San Francisco, I turned to reckon with my husband.

"I heard you," I told him, "when you were talking on your phone in the bathroom, while we were waiting for the shuttle back at the hotel."

With a cool stony gaze past me and out the window, he didn't even try to explain.

I added, "I don't know if there's any hope for this marriage. I don't know if I want to be with you anymore."

That evening we both walked silently into our home.

Maybe you're in a situation today that you didn't bargain for. Perhaps it's a job that seemed like a gift when you received it, but you discovered that it wasn't the right match for you. Or maybe a relationship feels irreparably broken. Whether the damage happened decades ago or you're suffering new disappointments today, you can't see how God is going to redeem it. I understand what it feels like to ask God, "Hey, what's going on here? What's Your plan here?"

If I could speak to that young Lisa today, I'd tell her what I'm telling you: *Hold on to God, because He has a plan for you.* No matter what is happening in your life, God is worthy of your trust.

Chapter 19

MOTHERING MY MOTHER

As a teen, whenever I'd slink home on Friday nights after a kegger at the river, my house would be full of strangers calling *my* mother "mom." And like any adolescent, I resented it mightily. So I'd creep in, keep my eyes to the ground, and make a beeline to my bedroom.

Twenty-five years later, my beautiful, faithful mother was still hosting prayer meetings.

As she'd done as long as I'd known her, Mom fasted every Friday as she sought the Lord in prayer. But at eighty-two, her body needed the food more than in the past. I encouraged her to try fasting from something else, but she was stubborn. And faithful.

One particular Friday when Faith was nine, Mom spent the night with us so she could see Faith's first cheer competition the next day.

My bedside clock glowed 2:52 a.m. when I was awakened by strange sounds. I heard what sounded like tortured moans, but I honestly couldn't tell if they were *human* sounds. Jumping out of bed, I rushed into the hallway, glancing through the open doorway into Faith's bedroom to find her sleeping soundly.

Pivoting to peek into the guestroom, I saw the door was open. Mom was not in there. She also wasn't in the guest bathroom.

I ran to the living room, which was still dark and quiet.

Running into the dim kitchen, I found my mother sprawled out on the hard beige travertine floor under the dining table. I skidded to her side on my knees to find her conscious but groggy.

"Mom, what's wrong?" I begged.

"I fell," she reported.

Glancing down at her pale blue pajama bottoms, I could see she'd wet herself, which was very unusual.

I helped support her as she stood up. Ducking under her arm, I eased her to the comfortable leather loveseat adjacent to the kitchen.

"Mom, I'm really concerned about you. I don't know what just happened, and I'd like to call 9-1-1."

As I heard the words leaving my mouth, I knew she would resist.

"No," she instructed firmly, "I'm just hungry!"

I was completely taken back when I heard her loud, unyielding tone. Although the self-sufficient attitude was familiar, her anger seemed out of character.

"Let me get you something to eat," I offered, still weighing calling for an ambulance.

In seconds I'd wiped peanut butter and jelly onto wheat bread, folded it in half, and poured a cold glass of chocolate milk, then I dragged a kitchen chair over to set beside her as an end table. She thanked me for the late-night snack and then ate in silence.

When she finished, I tried again to reason with her.

"Mom," I pled, "I really wanna call."

"No!" she barked again. "I'm fine."

I dropped the dishes into the sink, helped her up, and we walked back down the hallway. I washed her off in my master bathroom, and helped her into clean clothes. Still ambivalent about her condition, I asked her to sleep with me in the large bed that by then Deke was no longer sharing with me. Though reluctant, she agreed.

Even after her breathing slowed to a steady sleeping rhythm, I continued to lie awake, wondering what had just happened. I finally drifted off to sleep myself about an hour later.

But then I felt my mother stirring uncomfortably at my side. The movement startled me awake.

"Lisa," she said weakly, "I don't feel good. I think I'm gonna be sick."

She began to move to the far side of the bed.

I hopped up and grabbed the small trash can from my bathroom, ran around the bed, and held it below my mother's chin. All color had drained from her face as she dry heaved.

Now it was my call.

"Faith," I called out.

The clock now said 6:14 a.m.

"Faith!" I cried louder. "Wake up, honey, I need you."

A few seconds later a sleepy-eyed girl walked into my room.

"Remember when I told you about 9-1-1, and telling them our address? Now is that time," I instructed. "Can you go get the phone?"

Hearing the urgency in my voice, Faith grabbed the handset from the landline in the kitchen and dialed. Still holding and supporting my mom, I heard Faith give her name, our phone number, and our address.

"It's my grammy . . ." she began, then handed me the phone.

I explained to the operator that I'd found my mom after a fall about three hours earlier, and now she was vomiting.

Fourteen minutes later, when Faith opened the front door for a team of EMTs, my mom didn't use one ounce of her limited energy protesting.

As she was being gently lifted into the ambulance, I assured her, "After I get Faith settled, I'll be right there, Mom."

Another mother from the cheerleading squad agreed to watch Faith while I got Mom settled in the hospital. Thirty minutes later, I dropped Faith off at her house in her purple and white uniform. While Faith understood I wanted and needed to be in two places at once, I wasn't willing to abandon either my daughter or my mother.

When I got to the hospital, we were forced to wait for a treatment room to become available. My mom shooed me out, insisting I go to see Faith compete. When I arrived at the school hosting the competition, I climbed the bleachers to find a spot where I had a view of the entire gym. I felt like I was sitting on pins and needles throughout the entire event. The plastic smile on my face belied all the churning emotions inside me: pride in my girl and desperate worry about my mother.

As soon as Faith finished, we both zipped back to the hospital to check on Mom. She seemed a bit more like herself, and even requested a Subway sandwich, noting, "Albacore, please." Though I'd called her throughout the day, I was glad when the doctor arrived so I could get the report straight from him. He explained to me that she had had a minor stroke.

"When I found her on the floor," I explained with concern, "I just didn't know what had happened."

"I know," he said, "you didn't do anything wrong. Now for most strokes, patients who get what we sometimes call a 'stroke shot' within three hours have a very good chance of recovering."

"Oh my gosh," I gasped. "I just didn't know about that."

It actually sounded like I had done something very wrong by not calling 911 when I found my mom.

"No," he said in a more calming voice, "We actually found a little bleeder at the base of her brain. And when we see that, we can't give the shot."

Although I still hadn't heard any good news, I breathed a sigh of relief knowing that my hesitation had not compounded my mother's suffering. The doctor suggested Faith and I go home for the night, and that my mom stay so that they could do a few more tests in the morning. When we returned early the next day, my mom had been medicated but not permitted to eat until the tests were all done. But morning turned into afternoon—and when dinnertime came, I was really feeling a bit ticked off that she hadn't yet been made a priority.

At around 6:30 p.m., my mom started throwing up. I sent Faith to the nurse's station to get help, but as my mom was heaving, I watched her have another stroke. This one was much more serious, and impacted the entire left side of her body. I was furious. Although I don't know all the science behind what triggers strokes, I knew the hunger, as well as taking meds on an empty stomach all day, could not have helped.

A team rushed in to help, but because of the previous bleeder, they weren't able to give her the shot. When my mom regained consciousness, her left side was paralyzed and she was unable to walk or to talk. As she drifted in and out of lucidity, she persistently feared someone was choking her. The woman who was so excited to see her granddaughter cheer a day and a half earlier had been diminished in a multitude of ways.

I was scheduled to go on a Gaither tour two days later, and had no idea if I'd be able to leave. Feeling helpless and desperate, I called my pastor, Joel, and his wife, Georgia, to come pray for my mom. When they arrived, they offered hugs to everyone. When I saw Georgia pull anointing oil out of her purse, I knew they meant business. Inviting me and Faith to join them, they began to pray, moving around the room and anointing the whole space. Starting with the doorway, they prayed over the head and foot of my mom's bed and the doctors and nurses caring for her. Georgia gently made the sign of the cross on Mom's forehead using the anointing oil. It was a visible sign that God's blessing was upon her.

I begged the Lord to heal my mom's body. She was such a faithful saint, so committed to Christ and His kingdom, I reasoned, that if anyone should receive mercy, it would be my mom—even though I know it doesn't work like that. Beyond the decades she'd invested in those who circulated in and out of her prayer group, my mom had cultivated a rich private life of prayer with God. Because I'd seen her express it, I knew one of the gifts God had given her was speaking in tongues. When I'd sit beside her in church, I'd know she was about to blow when she began breathing deeply, in and out, in and out. Waiting. In and out, in and out. It almost felt like she wasn't willing to release herself to the Spirit unless she was convinced that it was Him roaring through her. Then, when it was time to channel the unintelligible words God gave her, it was like God pried open the top of her head and dumped it all in there! At times she would be given the gift of interpretation, and sometimes, others would interpret the words she had spoken.

As I listened to Pastor Joel praying for my mom in the Intensive Care Unit, something happened that I would not have believed if I hadn't seen it myself: my mother began speaking in tongues. And while I recognized her special prayer language, I certainly wasn't expecting it while she was laid up in a hospital bed unable to walk, talk, or feed herself! The strokes had left her with no control over her body. But it was like over the years she'd developed such a deep groove of obedience to God that not even the natural laws of health and science could prevent her from being used as His holy vessel.

If I ever doubted the Spirit of God to be real, I was never more of a believer than in that moment.

Thank You, Jesus. Your Word is true. Your promises are true. You are the one true God. You are the great I Am.

In those sacred moments, I had no idea whether my mother would live or die, but I knew she was held in the love of her Savior. That experience was a sweet kiss I'll never forget that built up my innermost faith—the faith I'd received from her.

My mom was released to a convalescent hospital to regain her strength day before I was scheduled to go on the road. So I knew she was in good hands. But on the fourth day of the tour, when I got a call saying my mom had to be rushed to the ER and readmitted to ICU, I hurried back home to help.

I wasn't weathering the crisis with the support of the husband who'd once loved me and my mom so well. Not only was I now doing it as a single mom, but a single mom whose work—to generate income to pay the bills—necessarily included travel. After the tour I was able to help my mom get settled back into the convalescent home. On any typical day I would juggle getting Faith ready for school, the duties of being an entrepreneur managing my own business, visiting my mom, and scheduling and keeping her doctors' appointments. And whereas Mom had been the president of my fan club, she now was having delusions, often upset that someone had come and kidnapped "the baby."

By the time Thanksgiving arrived, I'd begun taking Mom out of rehab for up to three hours at a time. She had a lot of physical needs, but on Christmas Eve, I busted her out for good to stay with Faith and me. That began a rigorous season of care that lasted over six months. Every day we'd welcome occupational therapists, physical therapists, and speech therapists. But because they couldn't book more than a week out, we could never settle in to a regular rhythm. I was organizing and offering my mother a host of new medications. She used adult diapers round the clock. After wheeling her into the kitchen or living room, I'd physically help her transfer to another chair.

Quite a bit later, when she'd improved a bit, my mom announced that she wanted to go home. I didn't blame her! Although she could get around with a walker, she would need help at home. So I researched in-home support services to piece together the kind of care she'd need to live semi-independently.

My friends and hers often praised me for the care I was giving her, but I always felt like there was more I could be doing. That woman is the reason I am still alive.

Never underestimate the power of a praying woman. They are *mighty*!

If you've had a mother, grandmother, or mentor who prayed for you, you know this. But beyond celebrating these powerful instruments of God's grace, I want to encourage you to *be* a powerful instrument of God's grace in the lives of others. What I learned from my mother was that it doesn't take a spiritual superpower to pray to God with faith in who He is and what He will do.

Does it take faith? Yes.

Does it take stillness? Yes.

Does it take discipline? Yes.

And because I've seen so many of my mother's prayers answered, I want to encourage you to get on your knees before God and pray big *prayers*. My mom taught me that nothing is too big for God. Nothing is too small. When you give yourself to God, with complete devotion, He is faithful.

When everything else had been stripped away from my mom, she never lost her direct communication with God. The Lord used that to teach me about what matters most in this life. Beauty fades. Bodies fail. Material gain can be lost. And we can even lose the relationships that matter most to us. But what we've invested in our relationship with the Lord can *never* be taken from us.

I have often thought God allowed me to see that powerful expression of faith in my mom in the hospital because I was going to need it. Even more was about to be stripped away from me.

Chapter 20

THE END OF A LOVE STORY

O n our tenth wedding anniversary, Deke and I renewed our wedding vows in a beautiful celebration at a historic downtown hotel, sharing dinner with about fifty friends. However, in the wake of that special weekend, several months went by without us being intimate. I'd wake in the middle of the night to find him sleeping on our leather couch in the living room or still "working" downstairs in the office. Eventually he started spending more and more time away from home, taking long weekends away to help his dad in Arizona when his father was no longer able to care for himself.

Over the next year, I began wonder if there could possibly be someone else in Deke's life. An accidental discovery on our home computer that matched our phone records confirmed my instincts were correct. When I confronted Deke, he didn't deny any of it.

It was like I was watching someone else's life unfold in front of me. There had been previous concerns about his fidelity, and we had attended counseling together in the past, but Deke showed no signs of wanting to prioritize our marriage. This time he felt ashamed to have been caught, and even sad for what we'd lost, but he made no offer to change. *Was divorce in our future?* Because the end of my parents' marriage had been so traumatic for me, Deke and I had always promised each other we'd never get divorced.

God, if You foreknew this, why did you allow me to marry this man? I struggled to assemble the disparate pieces of my life into any recognizable order. In the end, it was my mother, that holy saint of God, who helped me release those unanswerable questions. And to release Deke.

"Mom," I said one day over lunch, "I just can't get a divorce. I can't do that to Faith. But I also don't know what I'm supposed to do."

Because my mom is a loving, kind, gracious, generous woman who'd loved Deke for years as well as me, I knew she was right there with me in my struggle to hang onto the shreds of my marriage. So her response took me off guard.

Setting down her water, she looked me in the eyes and instructed, "Let. Him. Go. He has turned to idols. Let him go."

I don't know that I could have received those words from anyone else. She was faithful, she was fierce, and she was right.

Because it was clear that our marriage was beyond repair, I proceeded as I'd been advised to by a pastor I trusted: with a wonderful girlfriend at my side, I spent an entire day, tears streaming down my face, lovingly packing Deke's belongings into bins. I changed the locks on the front and back doors, which the pastor had recommended, and I wrote Deke a letter, placing the envelope on top of the stack of boxes just outside the front door.

Dear Deke,

This is certainly not what I want for our life. I don't understand what's going on, but I am willing to work through whatever we need to do to make this marriage strong. I love you with my whole heart, and I don't want our family shattered. I have packed some things for you at this time, and I'll be praying that you will be listening to what God is saying. You have been my rock on so many occasions, and I love you for that. I want you to know how much you mean to me. I hope you know how much I love you.

Lovingly,

Your wife.

The night when he came to pick up his things, I was at an event celebrating the release of a new CD. Graciously, one of the men who'd been counseling Deke was waiting there to support him. My friend stayed at our house that evening, and reported that Deke seemed broken and sad, but not really remorseful.

When I finally returned home that evening, I was surprised to see all he'd taken from our home. Too tired to be outraged, I paused in Faith's doorway to watch the peaceful rise and fall of her breathing as she slept. Walking to her bed, I dropped to my knees and laid my hands on her frame, silently begging God to protect her heart. Couches and guitars could be replaced, but I was also grieving the rupture my daughter was facing. She was already struggling to understand why daddy wasn't living with us, and waking up to a bombed-out shell of the only home she'd ever known wasn't going to help.

That humble, desperate posture I fell into beside Faith's bed, one of absolute dependence on God, was how I would survive. I didn't know what else to do.

The future I had seen so clearly in my mind's eye was suddenly unclear.

God, how did You allow this to happen?

Is it my fault? Am I responsible?

Will churches invite a divorced woman to perform?

Is my singing career over?

How will I provide for Faith?

Blindsided, I felt crushed by the trauma. For months I was disinterested in food, often unable to eat. During what I now look back on as a sacred season, I allowed God to nourish me with the good food only He can provide. Daily I feasted on His Word. The worship music that poured into our house every day trickled into my heart and soothed my parched spirit. Dry, desperate, I absorbed all God offered, and His overflowing tap kept me alive. Truly, I couldn't get enough of Him. The luxury of being nourished by His presence sustained me.

Whether I was loading the dishwasher, folding laundry, or dashing to the grocery store for milk, I was praying. It wasn't that God was loud or chatty or directive. He was simply available to me in the most palpable way I'd ever experienced.

The fact that the experience was somewhat novel was all on me! I was typically so active that slowing down to make time with the Lord had always taken effort and determination. But suddenly, I was content to do nothing more than bask in God's holy presence. I wasn't scrambling to accomplish anything. I wasn't trying to impress anyone. After getting Faith to school each morning I'd return home, stretch out on my bed, read God's Word, and let Him fill me with His peace and his comfort.

Almost two decades into my sobriety, I never *seriously* considered using drugs during that urgent season. But I was keenly aware that for much of my life I would have filled that kind of void with whatever satisfied: wine, champagne, vodka, weed, cocaine, valium—you name it. I was after whatever would numb me.

The sounds of Todd Agnew's song "Grace Like Rain" cascaded through our home during that season. Weaving the lyrics of "Amazing Grace" with fresh promises of God's abundant mercy, Agnew's delivery of "Hallelujah, grace like rain falls down on me" voiced the deepest cry of my own heart. I lapped up God's gracious mercy for me. For Faith. For Deke.

The morning after Deke ransacked our house, I pulled out my phone to snap pictures of it, room by room, before Faith woke up. It was a fitting metaphor for the ways my life was being ravaged. They were a stark contrast to the effusive posts I was seeing online about the success of my concert the previous evening celebrating my newest CD.

The song being released? "Forgiveness is a Powerful Thing."

Don't ever tell me God doesn't have a sense of humor. Little did I know when I penned that song that, on the night I released the album, I would learn what it really meant to live it out. Every day

I would be reminded that forgiving would have to be by God's power and not my own.

I was already paddling desperately to stay afloat financially, and I didn't know how much longer I could hang on before being pulled under. I was struggling to pay our monthly mortgage of thirty-two hundred dollars. And Faith's school tuition was another five hundred, on top of the rest of our expenses. And of course, caring for my mother and Faith made it more difficult to accept singing gigs and ministry dates. When Deke first left, he'd helped out with half the bills, but after a few months his commitment waned.

When the recession hit in 2008, I knew there was a possibility of losing our home. To learn more, I attended a conference at the Bank of America convention center.

"It really looks like you quality for an in-house loan modification," one banker assured me. "And if for some reason it doesn't work, you just make sure to get the paperwork in by May first, and we'll have about five other loans we can try."

Confident in that plan, I asked Deke to sign the quick deed so I could keep the process moving. He was in no rush, but I was, because the deadline was approaching. And each day that ticked by, *ticked me off.* Finally, on April 25, he said I could come by his apartment to pick up the signed documents. It was a relief to finally drive down to the bank and leave that envelope of completed paperwork with the banker who'd given me such hope just five days before the deadline.

But a week later, as Faith and I arrived home from a long day out, I found a notice taped to my front door announcing that the process of auctioning off my home was beginning.

"What's that, Mom?" Faith asked innocently.

What?! There had to be a mistake.

After skimming the first few lines, I pulled it off the door and assured her, "Nothin', baby, you don't have to worry about it."

Unlocking the door and throwing my bag on a chair, I said, "Go upstairs and start your homework and I'll call you when dinner's ready."

Dialing the bank's number, I asked to speak to the man who'd suggested they'd have a host of loan opportunities for me.

"I'm sorry," he said sincerely, "this is happening to a lot of people, and we're just not able to extend any more loans."

I could tell by his tone of resignation that any appeal would be futile.

Despite desperate networking to come up with the money needed to save the house, I simply couldn't do it. The very best I could manage was to get twenty-one days after auction to vacate our dream home. And that's about how long it took, even with hired help, to box everything up to move. Our garage was full of memories—and by "memories" I mean *stuff!*—from our twelve years of marriage, including all of Faith's baby things. We also had a recording studio full of equipment in the back. All we'd accumulated seemed endless.

As I was carrying a huge box from the living room out to the garage, where the essence of our lives was packaged in corrugated cardboard, I paused at the gate separating the yard from the driveway. When Faith had been about three years old, we'd had that concrete walkway poured, extending the driveway to lead all the way back to the studio. I'd held Faith while Deke pressed his handprint into the wet cement. Then he held her while I pushed my hand into the mixture. And then we made a final impression by gently pushing down on Faithbug's sweet little chubby hand.

When the first tear rolled down my cheek, I didn't even have a free hand to wipe it away. It landed between our three handprints. Our little family.

After dismissing the day's helpers and kissing Faith goodnight, I walked downstairs to our near-empty living room and fell to my knees.

"I don't understand, Lord," I began. "You knew I was always terrified of divorce."

My own parents' divorce had sent me spiraling, using alcohol and drugs for more than a decade to numb the painful feelings of rejection and abandonment. When Deke and I wed, we both intended to stay married, through hell or high water, until death did us part.

I knew I'd been complicit in the breakdown of our marriage.

And I was keenly aware of Deke's culpability.

But God was the one I'd trusted when we said "I do." I felt He shared some blame, too.

"You foreknew this would happen," I complained, "So why did You allow it?"

I wrestled mightily to understand God's ways. But nothing made sense.

"I feel alone!" I cried out. Then quickly added, "I know I'm not, but I don't understand how You have allowed me to go through the scariest thing in my life, the one thing I dreaded most, and to lose absolutely everything except my life."

I was no longer able to juggle all the balls I had. I was managing countless moving pieces as a woman in ministry, trying to figure out how to support my young daughter and aging mother. I had a book that was ready to pitch to publishers but that was dead in the water because there was no more story of "us." And we'd cycled through a string of caregivers in my mother's home who'd been caught lying and stealing. One harbored her heroin-using son there. During the ninety-day eviction process to get them out, my mother wasn't even able to return to her own home when she was released from the hospital.

What am I going to do?

Where am I going to go?

How am I going to accomplish all I need to do?

As I was crying out to God, He dropped a single word into my heart: *regardless.*

Though it came with absolutely no context, the Spirit interpreted it for me as I continued to pray words that also had to have come from God.

"No matter how I'm overlooked," I prayed, noticing a fresh conviction that clearly came from outside myself, "no matter how rough the terrain is going to get, I'm going to serve You *regardless.*"

I paused to absorb what I was simultaneously hearing and speaking.

"There's no turning back, Lord. I'm going to serve You—*regardless.*"

Even though I was being called to do something I didn't want to do in my natural flesh, that single word I'd heard from God—*regardless*—fueled my passion for the Lord. Regardless of any chaos that came my way, I would serve the Father Who loved me. It was as if all of the worries, stress, and responsibilities melted away and I was being given the gift of a single-hearted devotion to Christ.

As I continued to hold the word in my heart, I was given more words and phrases that became the lyrics to a song by the same name. The theme of the song was that no matter what happens, even the kind of darkness that had been blanketing me, I would trust and serve God.

If I had known a long time ago
Where I'd be right now.
Living this dream serving a king
And knowing I don't know how
To carrying this weight that I do today
Yeah anyone can see that it's not me ....
It's learning to believe
It's closin' my eyes to see
It's livin' down on my knees
It's knowin' where I will be
Through the fire, through the hardness,
Even in total darkness
I'm gonna serve: regardless.

When I'd lost almost everything I could lose, God never lost His grip on me. When I could no longer see, I was kept in God's sights.

Maybe today you are struggling to make sense of your circumstances. Perhaps your marriage has crumbled. Maybe you've lost a loved one to death. Or you may be battling an addiction or an illness. Know that no matter how dark the night seems right now, you are *seen*. You are heard. You are loved. When you can no longer see, God invites you to do what makes no sense: *close your eyes*. Seek His face. Listen for His voice. Discover His nearness. Regardless.

I know what it is to be completely undone, unable to see to take the next step. And if that's where you find yourself today, I want you to hear that you are not alone. If you have lost everything else, the Lord will never abandon or forsake you.

In time, God even restores what has been lost.

Chapter 21

SPRINGTIME

The next five years were chaotic. Faith and I were forced to move four times after I lost the house—even sharing a tiny bedroom at my mom's place for nine months. But eventually, things regained a sense of normalcy—even if it was a new kind of normal. I continued to hustle, and started dating a guy named Dub who'd been a family friend for years. He owned a rent house and offered me a great discount on it. Life settled back into a rhythm.

One Saturday night, four years after Deke left, I took Faith and her friend along on a trip to Paradise, California, where I'd be singing the next day. A group from the church went out for dinner together.

The church's worship team was amazing. One of the members—a man about my age—sang a beautiful rendition of "The Lighthouse" by the Hinsons. Though I'd heard this song at least a thousand times before, the voice of the man who sang it was absolutely captivating. Pure. Unique. Anointed. The way he worshipped God in that song was a blessing to me. I was so moved by and engaged by it that I began to weep. I found out later he was the pastor's brother, and his name was Ronnie Horton.

That evening we offered a concert at the church. It was set up a bit like the Homecoming Tour, inviting folks to sing along with us to all the old songs, like "The King is Coming," "He Touched Me," "I'll Fly Away," "In the Garden," and other various Gaither and Dottie Rambo songs. We all had a great time together. In fact, when the pastor started leading a few of the songs, Ronnie and I began harmonizing together. I was blown away by the incredible intonation of that voice. It was obvious this man was anointed by God.

After the concert, Ronnie and I started chatting, and it turned out we knew a lot of the same people. I made it very clear, however, that I was dating Dub and was faithful to him.

Six months later, I was performing in Rocklin, California, and Ronnie brought his nephew to the concert. It was a great evening, and the band and I really rocked out! As folks began to head home, Ronnie introduced me to his nephew—who plays drums in his band—and we got to chatting. When I mentioned I needed a soundman for a gig coming up in Paradise, Ronnie offered to help.

The next Saturday, he drove the ninety miles down from his home in Oroville, loaded up all my sound equipment, and took it all back up to Paradise. Not only that, but he enlisted the incredible soundman from his church to run sound for my band. It was an absolutely phenomenal gift. In Ronnie I saw a man who was willing to work as a servant for the sake of others and for the Gospel. After the Saturday outreach concert, he took me out for dinner, which was completely Christlike and innocent. And the next morning, leading worship at the same church where we'd met, I invited Ronnie to play guitar and sing a song. It was really fun performing together again with playful innocence.

Ronnie was becoming a Christian brother I trusted and enjoyed. While my on-and-off relationship with Dub was tumultuous—and at times excruciating—I was coming to discover that Ronnie was a consistent pillar of strength.

While my feelings were still platonic, Ronnie would admit—much later!—that his feelings for me were growing. Wanting to spend time with me, but also being very respectful of my relationship, he'd throw out offers like, "If you ever get hungry, give me a call." (I should have seen through that one!) Invariably, I *would* get hungry.

Dialing his number, I'd query, "What are you doing? I'm hungry."

I couldn't see him smiling on the other end, but I think he was.

So Ronnie would drive ninety miles to go out for burgers or a steak dinner. He said a lady who wasn't afraid to eat was endearing to him! And he was always a perfect gentleman. He'd open the door for me. He picked up the bill. And would offer only a quick hug goodbye when we parted.

As our friendship grew, I took note of what I was seeing. My boyfriend Dub was the one who'd taught me to observe someone's character over a long period of time. I'd learned that trust, born of repeated good behavior over time, was earned. And Ronnie Horton was earning my trust.

What I didn't know was that in addition to his growing feelings for me, Ronnie also was receiving guidance from the Lord. Whether or not we ever dated, Ronnie had a strong sense that God had called him to help me. At a performance one weekend, an evangelist called Ronnie out of the crowd to prophesy over him, saying in part, "God is telling me you have someone that has been on your heart, someone in the ministry that is in the throes of a battle. She is not alone, I have not forsaken her." Ronnie knew exactly who the Lord was speaking about. The preacher concluded by saying, "I am the Lord your God and I will make a way where there is no way. Trust Me, seek Me, and you will find My peace, the peace that passes all understanding, for I am God." Ronnie would continue to hold those precious words in his heart.

One weekend, I was asked to give a concert on a Friday night and lead worship for a women's ministry meeting in Mountain View, California. I left Faith with her father, and Ronnie went with me to help with the equipment.

The concert went well—but then my world was rocked to the core. Deke sent a text saying he had "something to do" and had left

Faith with a friend from his motorcycle club, the OG Riders. The fact that this group had ties to the notoriously criminal Hell's Angels wasn't lost on me.

I immediately called Deke to find out who this man was, and where he was keeping my daughter.

There was no answer.

Not any of the times I called.

I didn't sleep a wink that night. Being totally out of control, having no information, completely rocked with anguish about where my daughter was and what might be happening to her, was excruciating.

I finally reached a friend who was able to reach Deke, get the information, and pick up Faith from the unknown biker's house. But the incident weighed heavy on my heart all morning during the women's ministry event.

Afterward, Ronnie and I were breaking down the sound system and wrapping cords when a woman approached us. She looked to be about sixty years old, and asked us to come off the platform and join her down front. When we hopped off the stage, she pointed to the front row of chairs. The band had left and the sanctuary was nearly empty.

"I need you to sit in a chair in the front," she instructed me.

Not sure what was happening, I obliged. Ronnie dropped into the seat beside mine.

Looking me in the eye, serious but kind, she told me, "The Lord has a word for you."

Her announcement carried the same confidence I'd heard in my mom's voice over the years. The loving kindness the Lord had poured out on me through my mother gave me the confidence I needed to sit and receive God's word from a stranger.

Laying her hand on the top of my head, she began, "I've seen your sacrifice, I've seen your dedication and your faithfulness will not go unrewarded. God will rebuke the devourer and return to you what has been stolen."

The words felt like healing balm running down over my head.

She continued, "The Lord wants you to know that He knows your concern for your daughter."

She had my attention. More importantly, God had my attention.

"He knows," she continued, "and He says 'She was mine before she was yours. And I'm going to take care of her.' Fear not. I am with her. I will protect her."

The poignant personal words resonated with what I knew to be true of God throughout Scripture.

Tears streamed down my face. For a split second I wondered how on earth this woman could have known, but of course the Lord had shown her.

Gently lifting her hand from my head, she pivoted toward Ronnie. Laying that holy hand on his head, she also offered him a word that touched the most tender areas of his heart.

"This day," she announced, "I declare unto you the Lord your God has heard your prayers. I have seen the breaking of your heart and I know the longing you have to serve Me. This day I say to you, My son, 'I will give you a woman of song to stand by your side. You will see churches grow, your children and those you love will come to know Me . . . I say again, my child, I have heard your cries and I will answer,' saith the Lord."

We were both floored. After thanking the Lord for His kindness, we thanked the woman for hers. Although we'd come to give to this church, we left having received more from the Lord than we ever could have given.

Although Ronnie and I both believed that the Lord is faithful to speak to his children, and though we'd experienced God's guidance in the past, we learned it in a fresh way that day. When it's hard for us to see clearly, and when we struggle to hear God's voice, God is so gracious to make himself known to us in ways we can understand. Sometimes, as it was that day, God's speaks very explicitly. Other times God speaks more gently: through a Scripture, or the quiet internal nudging of the Spirit, or through the voice of a friend, or even through song lyrics! Beloved, know that the One who loves us is faithful.

Chapter 22

REDEMPTION

During that season my relationship with Dub was rocky. We'd break up for a few days, or a few weeks, but then get back together. Dub had a way of always dangling a carrot of hope before me. One on one, the relationship couldn't have been any sweeter. But once a crowd gathered, I became merely one of his dear friends. I felt completely manipulated, with my heart shattered, over and over again. This went on for five years. Broken promises, broken heart.

I didn't want to compare Ronnie and Dub, but it was difficult not to. In Ronnie I saw a man of character. He was consistent in his faith. He lived out his convictions. And although I didn't yet know the depth of his feelings, he had a steadfast love for me, his sister in the Lord.

I also didn't know that even though God was speaking to him about me, Ronnie was doing some negotiating himself.

"Lord, if she's going to keep going back to this guy, then release me," he'd pray. "I don't want to have these feelings if she's not ever going to be available."

Also during this season, Ronnie was investing time and energy into his own music. I learned that he and his family, who'd recorded five LPs, had traveled and performed together as the Horton Family

Singers. At every concert they'd take the stage in these fabulously groovy matching polyester bell-bottom suits. The Horton Family Singers had worked with the Hinsons and even opened for the Oakridge Boys. And now Ronnie was ready to record his own album.

He had a good friend, Gary "Bud" Smith, who'd played piano for Barbara Mandrel, Dolly Parton, Ricky Skaggs, and others, who kept encouraging Ronnie to record. If Ronnie provided the material, Gary promised to produce the album. I was excited for Ronnie, and wanted to help him make the most of that opportunity. Even though I was still seeing Dub, I offered to help Ronnie pick his best songs and suggest the current radio avenues that would give him his best shot. So he shared about twenty-five songs with me to get my opinions.

One afternoon I was listening to them, making notes on a yellow legal pad about which were the best, which could be shortened, how a lyric might be rhymed differently, which ones spoke to me, and which ones were radio-friendly and might be used in commercials. I was almost through evaluating them when Dub came over to pick me up for dinner. He knew Ronnie and I were friends, because there was nothing to hide.

"What's that?" he asked, as he noticed me pausing and re-starting the CD.

"I'm just giving Ronnie some feedback on some of his songs," I explained.

A change come across Dub's face. I'd begun to wonder if he felt a little threatened by my friendship with Ronnie, and his scowl now confirmed my suspicions.

"I don't want you playing with him anymore," Dub announced.

I couldn't believe the words I was hearing.

"What?!" I asked incredulously. "You don't want me to play music with Ronnie?"

In an instant, I was feeling all the feels: confusion, anger, sadness, surprise.

"That's right. I don't like it."

I couldn't help but muse that, when it came to spending time with other women, he had a different set of standards for himself. The rebel girl in me was outraged.

"Well you don't get to tell me what to do," I said plainly. "And I think you should go."

Though he looked like he was going to bark back at me, Dub turned abruptly and left.

It was clear that our relationship was in trouble. The things that once brought me the greatest joy, performing and recording and encouraging other performers, were seen by Dub only as things that took me away from him. He saw what I did as performing for attention, rather than ministry—which showed me that he didn't know my heart after all. He was always jealous, assuming more was going on than actually was. I can't say for sure how much that impacted my drive to keep doing what the Lord had called me to do, but I did know I was exhausted. I was done. I didn't want to sing anymore. Feeling like a shell of a person, I'd decided to start looking for a day job.

Later that week, when I told Ronnie about the lifelessness and fatigue I was suffering, he wasn't convinced it was time for me to stop singing.

"You have one more in you," he assured me.

If I was Moses, which sure felt like a stretch, Ronnie was my Aaron, keeping my arms raised when I'd lost the strength to do it myself. I finally moved out of the house we'd been renting from Dub, and with plenty encouragement from Ronnie, began collecting songs to record in Nashville.

I worked with producer James Bubba Hudson on the new release. He was a talented friend with whom I'd had the pleasure of working on "Forgiveness is a Powerful Thing." While that album had been more rockin', *Regardless* was more like a conversation. Among the songs I'd chosen was the one by that title, which I'd written during my darkest days. Bubba wasn't convinced it had what it took. We had to choose the strongest lineup of songs to record, and he didn't believe "Regardless" should make the cut.

"Really?" he asked. "You want to record 'Regardless'?"

Because of what the Lord had given me in that single word, there was no question in my mind.

"Yeah," I confirmed. "I really do. I need to record that one."

Reluctantly, he agreed.

Three days later, after we'd laid down the vocal, we played it back in the studio to hear the final cut. Glancing across the panel, I saw Bubba crying.

"I'm so glad we did this song," he said.

When we chose the tracks for the album, it was obvious the title had to be *Regardless*. The word and the comprehensive meaning it possessed was the umbrella over all the other songs on the CD.

Love found me, regardless.

Despite my mom's condition I'll worship, regardless.

No matter what my circumstances might be, I'll love God regardless.

As I was wrapping up my album, Ronnie suffered the loss of his longtime friend, Gary Bud Smith. Ronnie was shattered. Since Bud was going to produce his album, when he died, Ronnie's dream of recording almost did, too. But Ronnie had not let me give up on my dreams, so I wasn't about to let him give up on his.

One night we went out for dessert, and I could tell Ronnie was struggling with disappointment over not being able to record the way he'd always dreamed of.

"Get ready," I said, "We're gonna do your album!"

I'd hoped he'd light up with joy, but his face remained glum.

"I'm not ready," he said.

I'd heard other performers echo this sentiment. We want everything to be perfect before we record, but too often the commitment to perfection means that nothing happens.

I'd heard his stuff, and I knew Ronnie could do it.

"You're ready," I countered. "And I got this. I'm gonna produce this."

"No," he insisted again, "I'm really not ready."

I can be pretty persuasive when I want to, and I had no intention of dropping it. Ronnie must have known that.

"Yes," I said with a tone of finality, "You're going to do this. I'm going to do this for you."

I introduced Ronnie to some of the best players I knew, and four weeks later, we were in the studio. What came out of those sessions was absolutely beautiful.

After the long, series of starts and stops, I finally closed the door on Dub. He'd never supported my ministry, always telling me, "You don't have to sing anymore. You can do one benefit concert per year." Even though Dub would continue to reach out to me, even inviting me to go away with him, I remained firm in my resolve. I knew if I returned to him, the cat-and-mouse game would continue. My heart had been shattered and I wasn't willing to turn back to a slight "maybe." I refused to be played anymore.

I was invited to be a judge on a series of talent shows hosted by the Inspirational Country Music Association called *The Nashville Talent Search*. It was a privilege to serve alongside Buddy Jewel, Jeff Bates, and Chuck Day. It gave me joy to identify and encourage young talent. Ronnie traveled with me to a few of the showcases, emceeing the events, and we always had a great time together. He was so funny and was always making me laugh. He was also wise, and I could count on receiving good counsel whenever I needed it. Because of my history with men, it had become hard for me to trust them. But gradually, that broken part of me was being rebuilt with Ronnie. Hour by hour, day by day, he proved himself to be trustworthy

Ronnie continued to help me at gigs. He'd help set up on the front end and load up on the back end. He'd play guitar. He'd encourage me. As our relationship continued to grow, I knew that Ronnie wanted more. One evening after we said goodbye and I'd come home, kissed a sleeping Faith, and settled into bed, a single question filled my mind.

Is this someone I want to live my life without?

I didn't have to weigh anything because the answer was clear: NO. I wanted Ronnie in my life. I already loved him as a Christian brother, but I began to pray that God would put the kind of love in my heart that a wife has for a husband. During the six years I'd been observing his character, I'd discovered who he was. He loved God first, and me as a very close second. He was super funny. He was wildly intelligent, in business and life. He fixed things with his own hands, rather than hiring others to do it. He'd built several houses. Passionate about sharing the Gospel of Jesus Christ, he loved and clung to truth. And, although I would never have wished it for him, he knew what it felt like to be betrayed, to lose everything, and to rebuild a life from the ashes. He had that beautiful rare voice, as well as being a skilled guitarist and songwriter. And did I mention he adored me? What more could a girl want?

The weekend of Ronnie's birthday, we gathered family and friends for a party on Saturday afternoon. Then on Sunday evening, he took me to one of my favorite restaurants in Tahoe, The Ciera Steakhouse inside of Montbleu Casino. Always generous, he encouraged me to really splurge, so I ordered my favorite item from their menu—steak and lobster. Dinner was exquisite, and when we finished, I noticed that the man who's usually pretty slick was fumbling with something I suspected might be a ring.

I'm not even going to pretend I didn't start acting like a control freak. If he was going to propose, I didn't want him popping the question in a casino.

"Let's go to the beach and watch the sunset," I suggested, dragging him outside.

It was a beautiful evening in late July, and we sat on a bench, enjoying the peaceful beauty of Lake Tahoe. Tahoe really is my happy place, and being there with Ronnie made everything in the world seem *right*. Minutes later we watched the shining orange orb drop behind the mountains.

On the heels of the radiant sunset, Ronnie pivoted in front of the bench and dropped to one knee.

Looking into my eyes, he began, "Lisa Daggs, I am in love with you and I don't want to live the rest of my life without you."

His words reminded me that I'd recently realized the same thing.

With what appeared to be a mingling of joy and nerves, he opened a jewelry box holding a shiny engagement ring, and asked, "Will you marry me?"

Without hesitating, I burst out, "Yes! Yes I will!"

What more could I ask for? He was a man of God who knew and loved the Word. He'd never used alcohol or drugs. He had that incredible voice and talent from the Lord. And he loved me. He loved me a *lot*. Yes!

We were married two and a half months later, on October 7.

Ronnie and I continue to perform together and, if it's possible, there is a fresh anointing on stage we've noticed since we've been married. Truly, sometimes we get goosebumps when God's Spirit moves in that deeper way. God has given us this ministry together.

I am finally home.

From what he says and what I experience, Ronnie's love for me has only grown since our marriage. I can be sauntering around in yoga pants and a sweaty T-shirt, rocking a messy bun on my head, and he'll call out after me, "You're beautiful and I love you." And if there's a day when he's not had the opportunity to say it, he reminds me before we drift off to sleep at night, "I love you. And you're beautiful."

For years, I asked myself why I hadn't been enough. For my dad. For Deke. For other men. But with Ronnie, I live grounded in the reality that I am enough, and *more*. I feel whole. And I don't mean that Ronnie has filled the void in my heart that God is meant to fill. I mean that he reflects for me the steadfast love God has for me that has always been, even when I couldn't feel it.

Over the years, God has also blessed my career. I sang the national anthem at a Sacramento Kings game to over twenty thousand fans.

I've been voted both Entertainer of the Year and Female Vocalist of the Year by the Christian Country Music Association (CCMA) as well as Entertainer of the Year by the Inspirational Country Music Association. To date I've released nine full-length CDs, plus several others. I've had twenty-one Number One singles. I'm on the road performing over fifty concerts a year, either with Ronnie or with my band.

The most important moment of each concert is when I get to share the testimony of what God has done in my life. What I want every audience to hear is simply the way God has reordered it: "God is so good. He's given me back the desires of my heart. I love the Lord with all my heart, and then my family, and then the ministry—that's the order today."

If you were asked to share today about what God has been up to in your life, what would you say?

Perhaps you are living hard, like I once was. Maybe you've suffered losses and disappointments. Maybe you can't see how God could ever love you or use your life for His glory. I get that. But I want you to expect the miracle. Expect the unexpected. Because our God is that big. Though it can feel as if He's absent in your suffering, He knows and cares about the details of your life. Whether the electric bill has been paid. Whether you still carry a childhood wound in your heart. Whether a particular guy ever called you like he said he would. Or not. Like the many Friday nights I waited for *that* call. Nothing that matters to you is outside God's sight or hearing.

Maybe you've given your life to God, and you're still facing hardship. You need a job that pays more money. You are concerned about choices your children are making. You're lonely and waiting for Him to send your life partner. You're facing an illness you can't manage on your own. I feel you. I was feeling that low and empty when Faith and I were being evicted from our home. I felt my daughter's broken heart. I felt it when Faith and I had to move four times in five years. I felt it when we shared a ten-by-ten-foot room back at my mom's house for nine months. When I was at my lowest, God sent a single word to inspire me to keep doing what I'd been created to do: *regardless*.

If you've suffered from the choices you've made, if you've exhausted your own resources, if you can't see what's next, I invite you to live wholeheartedly for God.

Worship, regardless.

Serve, regardless.

Trust, regardless.

Beloved, there is nothing in this whole world—not alcohol, not drugs, not broken relationships—that can separate you from the love of God in Jesus Christ. And as one who is fearfully and wonderfully made, you have been created to use your gifts, whatever they may be, for the sake of His kingdom. I promise you that when you give yourself to the Lord with abandon, He will use your life for His glory.

Regardless.

If I had known a long time ago where I'd be right now
Living this dream, serving a King and knowing I don't know
  how
To carry this weight, that I do today, yeah anyone can see
That it's not me.
It's learning to believe
It's closing my eyes to see
It's livin' down on my knees
It's knowing where I will be

Through the fire, through the hardness
Even in total darkness,
I'm gonna serve,
No turning back
Regardless